My Children Are Friends With Jesus

John 15:15 «I no longer call you servants...
Instead, I have called you friends. »

Gabriel Marcelin

Published by Gabriel Marcelin www.heavenlycitizen.shop

Contact: heavenlycitizenshop@gmail.com

ISBN (Paperback): 978-1-0696534-0-6
ISBN (Hardcover): 978-1-0696534-1-3
ISBN (Ebook): 978-1-0696240-9-3

Dedication

*Jesus said, "The **kingdom of heaven belongs to every child."***

To **every child around the world.**

To the children who already **know His love**, and to those still waiting to **READ** it for the very **first time.**

May you grow stronger in your faith and walk closely with Him.

To those who are just beginning the journey of faith, **reading this book and learn about Jesus.**

It is a significant **first step** in meeting the best Friend you'll ever have.

To every child without a **mommy or daddy, you** *are not forgotten.*

God sees **you**, He knows **your name**, and loves you more than you can imagine.

You are His **precious child**, and He will **never leave you**.

Always remember this:
You are loved. You are chosen.
You are never alone.
Jesus is with you
He calls you his friend.

With love and prayers, we wish you good reading.

From: Gabe Jr., Isaiah, Gershom, and Olivia.

Table of Contents

Introduction

Did you know that **millions of children** worldwide have never heard or read about **Jesus?**

Every chapter in this book shows that no kid should be left behind or too small for God to use. Jesus said: "**Let the little children come to me**... because God's **kingdom of Heaven** belongs to them." (Matthew 19:14)

That means you and I will tell them about the greatest Friend who has ever lived. They don't know how much Jesus loves them or how He died and rose again to save them. He wants to walk with them every day. But guess what? **Kids like you can help make a difference!**

This book is filled with stories about children just like you, Christian children with big hearts, strong faith, discipline, and a love for Jesus that shines in everything they do. You'll read in every home about:

- Friends who help others with a big heart and ask, **'What Would Jesus Do?'**
- **Families that are friends of Jesus, where prayer, love,** and kindness fill the home.
- **Children who learn to listen and obey parents and teachers,** softening their wild hearts by following Jesus' words.

- **Heroes like Daddy, the 68W medic**, who helps others in war and peace, and serves Christ with courage
- **Truth-telling kids**, who are honest, brave, and trustworthy, because Jesus lives in their hearts

And you'll even learn how **your home can be a healing place**, full of prayer, peace, and play.

Jesus loves children of all races, countries, and backgrounds. When you follow Him through your words, actions, and heart, you become a bright light for the world, like a city on a hill visible to everyone. Let your light shine by doing good so others see and **praise God in heaven**.

So, come and read together with Jesus. Be bold. Be kind. Be honest. Be brave. **Never forget, your story matters to Jesus.**

Chapter One

My children are friends with Jesus

We belong to the kingdom of heaven, and we must listen to your parents or grandparents.

HEAVENLY CITIZEN

My name is **Isaiah**, and my family has a profound love for Jesus. **I Am a Friend of Jesus.**

I am a child, just like you. I go to school, play games, and have friends. But there is something very special about me: I am also a friend of the Lord Jesus.

Not all of my friends share my faith in Jesus. Some even say they don't believe in Him at all. Initially, I wondered **why I wouldn't want to believe in the One who loves us, helps us, and offers eternal life?** But then I understood something crucial: they don't think so because they haven't yet come to know Him.

The Bible says, *"How, then, can they call on the one they have not believed in? And how can they believe in the one of whom they have not heard?"* (Romans 10:14). People cannot believe in someone they do not know. That is why it is so essential for my brothers, Gabe and Gershom, and me, as children of God, to share who Jesus is with our friends.

Jesus' story started in **Bethlehem**, where He was born to Mary and Joseph in a simple family. Angels sang the good news of His birth, and shepherds came to see the baby who would be the Savior of the world.

As He grew, Jesus lived in **Nazareth**, His childhood home. There, he had brothers, sisters, and friends. He learned to work as a carpenter's son, helping Joseph with wood and tools. More than anything, He grew in wisdom and in favor with God and people, quietly preparing for the mission God had given Him.

When the time was right, Jesus went to the **Jordan River**, where His cousin John the Baptist **baptized Him**. At that moment, the heavens opened, the Holy Spirit descended like a dove, and God's voice declared, "This is my beloved Son, in whom I am well pleased." From there, Jesus started His ministry.

Have you been baptized?

Baptism is a special act in which a Christian is immersed in water to demonstrate their belonging to Jesus. It signifies that their old life is washed away, and they now live a new life as a child of God.

Jesus traveled through **Capernaum and Galilee.** Wherever He went, He preached the good news of God's Kingdom, healed the sick, calmed storms, and called His 12 disciples, who would follow Him and learn from Him. Crowds gathered to hear His words because they were filled with truth and love.

At the end of His time on earth, Jesus took His disciples to the **Mount of Olives**, near Bethany. He blessed them, promised that the Holy Spirit would come to help them, and then He ascended into heaven. *"And while they beheld, he was taken up; and a cloud received him out of their sight"* (Acts 1:9).

And so, Jesus, the best friend of all children, began His story on earth with love and ended it with a promise: *that He would never leave us and that one day, He would come again.*

When was the last time you **blessed someone**? You might be wondering, *"How can I bless somebody?"*

Blessing someone doesn't always mean giving a **big gift**; it can be as simple as sharing what you have or showing kindness. Maybe you gave your friend half of your sandwich when they forgot their lunch, or you helped your little sister clean up her room, or do her homework. **That's a blessing!** Sometimes a **smile, a hug**, or kind **words** of encouragement are just as powerful as giving something material. Every time you help, share, or show love, you are **blessing someone** the way God wants us to.

Jesus said that all children are precious to Him, and He calls them His friends. When we are friends with Jesus, we are never alone. He walks with us, listens to us, and cares about everything in our lives. Jesus even told His disciples, *"Let all children come to me, for my kingdom of heaven belongs to them"*. This means that every child is welcome in their family and is deeply loved by God.

We are **three brothers**, and we are proud to say that we are friends of Jesus. Being His friends means we are also called Christians, just like the disciples long ago.

The Bible tells us: *"The disciples were called Christians first at Antioch"* (Acts 11:26). Even the great Apostle Paul, who taught people about Jesus everywhere he traveled, was a Christian. When we call ourselves Christians, we are saying that we belong to Jesus and want to live like Him.

This book will help us read and learn together about God's plan for every child. Jesus has a special purpose for each of us, and His teachings show us how to love, forgive, and live with joy. He is the best friend of all friends, the kind who never leaves, who always forgives, and who promises to be with us forever. Walking with Jesus is the most incredible adventure we could ever have!

All **Christian children** should have a trusting heart. Any child can be friends with Jesus by believing in Him and trusting that He is God's Son. Jesus is not looking for **perfect** children, but for thoughtful hearts. Jesus says, *"He loved all children, for the kingdom of God belongs to them"* (Matthew 19:4).

Jesus does not push children away; he draws them to himself. *Children are very special in his eyes, because their faith is straightforward, honest, and full of wonder.* Believing in Jesus means trusting that he loves you, that he died for your sins, and that he wants to be your friend forever. Even if you don't understand everything, Jesus sees your heart, and that's what matters most.

John 15:15:

"Jesus said, I call you my friends, because I have told you everything my Father told me."

Then people brought little children to Jesus, so He could lay His hands on them and pray for healing. Jesus laid His hands on them, and He healed and blessed all the children.

Jesus called all children, boys and girls, His friends, and said: "**They all belong to the Kingdom of Heaven**". One day, all children will see Jesus in person in Heaven, but for now, we must pray every day, do good things for one another, and be kind to everyone, regardless of their origin or the color of their skin.

If you welcome and care for a child as you would for Me, it's like you are welcoming Me."(Matthew 18:5)

When we show kindness to other children, Jesus will bless us in wonderful ways. He helps us excel in school, earn good grades, and achieve our dreams. Plus, Jesus sends special messages to our parents. That's why my parents pray every day, asking Jesus for His blessings and protection for us.

Jesus teaches us to be kind and polite to everyone, *regardless of their background or appearance*. **All children belong to the same God and the same heavenly Kingdom.** Jesus was once a boy, too, and even though He was brilliant, He was always gentle and loving toward everyone.

One day, in the beautiful city of Jerusalem, Jesus preached to the people about the importance of always treating others with kindness and compassion. This teaching is known in the Bible as **The Golden Rule of**

God, which means "Treat others the way you want to be treated, like a friend, brother, or sister, not a bully.

If you're good at math and a friend excels at science, we can support each other and strengthen our friendship! Every child has an angel in heaven watching over them. My angel observes everything I do. That's why my family feels blessed, because we follow Jesus' teachings to show kindness to everyone.

We did our best to stay out of **trouble at school**, knowing that misbehavior would only bother our parents and force them to leave work for meetings. By acting out, we would have taken them away from their duty to care for and provide for us at home. Instead, we learned to do our part **by being responsible** and striving to be good.

Remember to treat *all children with kindness and respect*. They are like angels and constantly have a special connection with Heaven. Let's value and safeguard the gentle innocence and happiness of every child.

Generational blessings, do you know what that is?

Generational blessings are wonderful gifts and favors from God that are passed down through the generations, from our grandparents to our parents, and then to us. God reminds us in Proverbs 13:22, "A good man leaves an inheritance to his children's children," which means more than just material wealth. It includes character, faith, and a lasting legacy. When your parents pray, Jesus can activate blessings that will benefit all children and grandchildren, creating a beautiful ripple of divine favor throughout your family.

Many years ago, in the beautiful country of **Israel**, a king named David made a significant change to the country's capital. **He renamed the capital from Hebron to Jerusalem**, which has remained the capital to

this day.

Do you wish to visit?

His son became king after him. His name was King Solomon, who built a magnificent temple in this city, where the Ark of the Covenant is kept, a sacred, gold-covered chest. This was a divine secret, entrusted by God to His faithful servants, such as **King David and King Solomon**. They are father and son. Additionally, the grandson of King David, the son of Solomon, Rehoboam, succeeded his father as king.

King **David** led God's people with courage, guiding and teaching them to trust in the Lord. He was also a musician who played the harp. His son, King Solomon, demonstrated his love for the people by seeking wisdom from God to make just decisions and maintain the nation's strength. Rehoboam, Solomon's son, also became king to lead and protect the people. Each of these kings was chosen to love and care for God's children, showing that leaders should serve with kindness and follow God's ways.

What happens if you don't listen to your parents Or grandparents?

Let's examine the kings of Israel. **King David** was brave and faithful, uniting all of God's people as one strong family. His son, King Solomon, was a wise and wealthy man who built the Temple of God.

King Solomon built a beautiful **temple for God in Jerusalem**, on **Mount Moriah**. It was called *Solomon's Temple or the First Temple*. This temple was very special because it was the place where all of God's children came to worship, pray, and offer sacrifices. Inside, everything was made with the finest materials: gold, silver, and fine wood, because Solomon wanted to give God the very best. The temple demonstrated to the people that God was with them and that His house was at the heart of their lives.

1 Kings 4:29–30:

"God gave Solomon wisdom and very great insight, and a breadth of understanding as measureless as the sand on the seashore. Solomon's wisdom was greater than the wisdom of all the people on the planet."

Solomon's son, **King Rehoboam, didn't listen to wise advice from his dad,** and because of that, the kingdom broke into two parts, and the people didn't live happily together anymore. This is why your parents remind you to behave well, be kind to everyone, be respectful, and be thankful, because wise choices help keep families and friendships strong.

Chapter Two
Showing respect for parents

Obedience in God's Family

HEAVENLY CITIZEN

Children should show respect for their parents.

There was a man named Paul, also known as the Apostle **Paul**. He was a writer, a brilliant thinker, and a teacher who gently reminded us that children should obey their parents in all things. This means listening carefully and doing what our parents ask us to do, helping us grow and learn together.

God gave our parents a very special responsibility: to guide, teach, and care for us. When we obey our parents, we demonstrate that we trust God's plan for our family. Part of that plan includes respecting the wisdom and care God has entrusted to our parents.

Obeying our parents isn't just about following rules; it's about building trust and love within our family. This is what Apostle Paul wrote in the Bible.

Colossians 3:20.

"Children, always listen to your parents and do what they ask you to do. This pleases God." **Obedience as an Expression of Love for God and My Parents."**

When kids obey their parents, it's more than just following rules or avoiding trouble. It's really about obeying God! Jesus tells children to respect and honor their parents, because when they do, they are following God's plan for their lives.

In Ephesians 6:1-3, the Bible promises that when you obey your parents, things will go well for you, and you will have a long, happy life on Earth. *Jesus will make sure you live longer here.*

So, when you listen to your parents, you not only make them happy but also show love and respect to God, who gave your parents the critical responsibility of caring for you. Your parents will be very proud of you.

My parents are Jesus' representatives in our home, and they are responsible for caring for me and all the children in our family. When I obey them, I show respect and love for them. Without my parents providing me with a place to sleep, a safe home to return to after school, food to eat, and a space to play, I would be in a difficult situation. For all these things, I am thankful and love my mommy and daddy for their hard work in taking care of me. From now on, I vow to listen to and obey my parents, and to tell them how much I appreciate and love them.

Obedience in God's Family

Obedience to parents is one of the first and most important lessons learned in childhood. As people grow, they face situations that require making decisions and facing challenges. At this point, parental support becomes especially vital. Building the habit of obedience and respect for our parents in all matters lays a strong foundation for making wise choices and respecting authority throughout life.

Furthermore, **my family was the first place where I experienced God's love and learned important lessons from my parents**. The teachings of Jesus guide me to respect my parents and follow God's Word. Because of this, obeying my parents becomes a meaningful part of my lifelong journey to follow God's will, bringing me fulfillment and peace.

King Solomon said in Proverbs 1:8-9:

"Listen, my son, to your father's instruction and do not forsake your mother's teaching. They are a garland to grace your head and a chain to adorn your neck."

This means that when you listen to the wise advice your parents give you, it's like putting on a *beautiful crown and a shiny necklace*. Just as a crown makes you look special, following your parents' teachings makes your heart and life lovely.

Parents' wisdom will guide you to make wise choices, stay safe, and grow into a kind and wise person. You will also have Jesus' grace in your life to help you succeed in school. So, every time you listen to and learn from your parents, it's like putting on something that makes you shine, feel good, and look beautiful.

"Do you know why Jesus loves children so much?"

Mommy asked as she sat with my little brother, Gershom, on the couch. **"Why?"** said little brother Gershom, with his eyes wide open with curiosity. **"Because children are special to Jesus. He loves how pure and trusting you are. He wants you to be close to Him, like we want to be close to each other."** Mommy replied with a gentle smile. **"Jesus is the only person in the whole world who can see into every child's heart and mind to know how good we are."**

We love everyone; we do good to each other, right, mommy?" *Gershom nodded, feeling the warmth of her words.* "That's right, my baby boy," **she said.**

Matthew 19:14:

Jesus' words, "Let the little children come to me, and do not hinder them, for the kingdom of heaven belongs to such as these."

Daddy, on the other hand, is the family's teacher; he taught us something just as important. He said, "**When we're sad or feeling sick, we need to share our thoughts with our family,**" he would say. "That way, we can pray together to ask Jesus for good health and comfort."

Mommy agreed, adding, "In any good family, **there are no secrets.** We need to be open like a book with lots and lots of stories so that we can help each other." Gershom smiled, thinking about the love and care that surrounded him, both from his family and from Jesus.

Mommy's name is **Zipporah**, and Daddy's name is **Moses**. I have a big brother named **Gabe**, and I have a little brother named **Gershom**. We're a happy family, and even though we're very close, there's another special girl in our family, a little cousin named **Olivia**.

We love her so much! My **grandpa's name is Faustin**, a wise and funny man who loves to tell us stories about **Jesus**. He's a preacher, a gentle servant of Jesus who always speaks softly and lovingly.

Grandpa is also the most pleasant person to be around. He constantly invents new games for us to play, keeping us entertained and making us laugh along the way. He has some fantastic stories about all of his children. He told us that once, Mommy was very sick, and Grandpa prayed to **Jesus** for her to get better.

And guess what? Jesus heard his prayers and healed Mommy!

Jeremiah 33:3:

"Call to me and I will answer you and tell you great and unsearchable things you do not know."

Jesus as the Child of God

From the very beginning of His life on earth, Jesus knew He was the Son of God. Even as a boy, He understood that God had a special mission for Him. When his parents found him in the temple at twelve years old, Jesus told them, "Didn't you know I had to be in my Father's house?" (Luke 2:49). This shows that Jesus always put his heavenly Father first and lived as a true child of God.

Honoring Earthly Parents. Although Jesus knew He was God's Son, He still showed respect and obedience to His earthly parents, Joseph and Mary. The Bible says, "He went down with them and was obedient to them" (Luke 2:51). This teaches us an important lesson: listening to and honoring our parents is not a sign of weakness; it is an expression of love. Jesus demonstrated that by respecting our parents, we also honor God's plan for families.

Jesus cares deeply for children! His love comes from His nature and the mission given to Him by God. Children possess qualities that please God: humility, innocence, and trust. When the disciples tried to prevent children from approaching Him, Jesus said, "Let the little children come to me. Don't hinder them, because the Kingdom of God belongs to people like them" (Mark 10:14). Jesus loves children because their hearts are sincere and open, eager to believe and follow Him.

Children as Models of Faith

Jesus even told adults to learn from children! He said, "Anyone who will not receive the kingdom of God like a little child will never enter it" (Luke 18:17). What does that mean? Grown-ups often make life complicated with pride, worries, and doubts. But children know how to trust, depend on others, and stay humble. That's why Jesus loves children so much; their simple, trusting hearts are precisely what God wants from everyone who follows Him.

Because Jesus loves children so much, He strongly warned adults about how they treat them. Jesus said that anyone who hurts or misleads a child who believes in Him is doing something serious in God's eyes (Matthew 18:6).

This highlights the special place children hold in God's eyes. Caring for them is a big responsibility. Adults are called to protect children, help them learn about God, and guide them in the right way.

Jesus loves children because they embody the heart of His mission: to bring people into God's eternal family. Everyone, whether kids or adults, is invited to become a child of God by trusting in Jesus. Children remind us how we should all live: trusting God as a Father, rejoicing in His love, and feeling safe in His care. In God's Kingdom, a child's faith is not minor; it's one of the greatest treasures of all.

Chapter Three

I Speak Honestly Because I Am a Friend of Jesus

I love Christmas! And you, which holiday do you prefer?

HEAVENLY CITIZEN

I believe in being truthful, brave, and trustworthy. These qualities are essential to me and help me genuinely connect with others.

Jesus teaches *all children* always to tell the truth to their parents, because telling the truth makes our hearts clean and brings peace to our homes. In the Bible, Jesus says, *"Then you will know the truth, and the truth will set you free"* (John 8:32). When I tell the truth, I feel free inside my heart. It keeps me safe and helps my parents trust me more and more every day.

I always tell Mommy and Daddy the truth, because I am a child of God. You do the right thing when you're honest. Jesus says, **"Children, obey your parents in the Lord, for this is right."** (Ephesians 6:1). Obeying and telling the truth makes Jesus very happy with me. I know that God made me *beautiful and bright*. I am intelligent, and I can do all the good things Jesus put into my mind, who gives me strength.

Philippians 4:13:

"With Jesus helping me, I can do anything He wants me to do."

I tell the truth at home, at school, to my friends, and my brothers and sisters. My little brother, Gershom, always tells me the truth, too, and we help each other do what is right. When we speak the truth, we make Jesus smile because He loves honest hearts.

My daddy showed me this *verse in the Bible: "The Lord detests lying lips, but Jesus delights in people who are trustworthy" (Proverbs 12:22).*

No one at school can bully me, make me feel sad, or frighten me, because I know **who I am**. I am a Christian; my siblings and all my friends are friends of

the Lord Jesus. He loves me and watches over me.

Hebrews 13:6

"The Lord is my helper; I will not be afraid. What can man do to me?"

So, I stay strong and kind, and I ignore people who try to be mean. Jesus is my best friend, and He teaches me to forgive and love everyone, even those who are unkind.

I will always tell the truth because it keeps my heart pure, brings joy to my family, and helps me stay close to *my best friend, Jesus.* I am proud to be honest, because I am a child of God, the King of all! *I matter. I am special.* I am worth so much to *myself* and *my God.* He made me bright, full of wisdom, and capable of **understanding wonderful things.**

I respect everything God created. When I look at the sky or think about the world around me, I remember that Jesus' **light** is always there. The world never really goes dark. *The Sun is always shining somewhere*, because the Earth is a large planet that orbits the Sun. This means the Earth is a spherical planet that orbits the Sun in space. It makes a big trip in a circle, *taking one whole year to go all the way around*, moving at a super-fast speed of about 40,000 kilometers per hour. When it's night here, it's daytime on the other side of the world, and some of that sunlight reflects into our sky.

The Moon doesn't produce its light; it reflects the Sun's light. The stars are very far from the sun, and their light travels across space to reach us. Jesus, the wisest and most loving One ever, made sure we always have some light. And you know what? Children everywhere are like little lights to every country in the world, shining brightly for Him. As friends of Jesus, we are the sunshine that brightens the world's future.

I love Christmas! And you, which holiday do you you prefer?

In 2024, my whole family travelled to Boston, Massachusetts, USA, to celebrate Noël together. We all flew into Logan Airport and stayed at a beautiful hotel.

The InterContinental Hotel, situated in the heart of downtown Boston, is adjacent to South Station, a central transportation hub serving buses, trains, and subways. The city was covered in fresh snow and decorated so beautifully for the holiday season; *Noël songs were everywhere*; it felt just like stepping into a Christmas movie.

One of the highlights of our trip was visiting "*The Boston Common*" and the Public Garden, which had been transformed into a dazzling winter wonderland filled with sparkling holiday lights. **The State House, located in Beacon Hill and standing proudly above the Common**, looked especially stunning against the snowy backdrop. At its center was a massive Christmas tree, a generous gift from Nova Scotia, Canada, glowing brightly in the night.

At first, my little brother **Gershom** wasn't pleased because he was cold. I gave him my gloves to warm his hands, and once he felt better, he loved ice skating at the famous Frog Pond, a skating rink in the middle of the Common. Surrounded by the city skyline and twinkling lights, it was a **classic Boston Christmas experience**. Many families from all over the world visited, and children skated together, making it a lot of fun.

On Saturday, December 28, 2024, we all got tickets to see **The Nutcracker** performed **by the Boston Ballet at the Opera House**. It was **pure magic**, feeling like stepping into a fairy tale, and created an unforgettable holiday tradition for families and visitors alike. Of course, we couldn't miss **Faneuil Hall Marketplace**, where we discovered many delicious food options, perfect for warming up after a day out in the cold. That was Gershom's favorite place; he loved the food so much that he wanted to return just for the cozy atmosphere and tasty treats.

During our time exploring Boston, we befriended some children visiting over the holidays. We are from

Montreal, Quebec, and they are from Jacksonville, Florida. It was special and meaningful to *discover that they are also friends of Jesus, just like us*. We shared a magical experience riding the Polar Express, a short train ride nearby that made us feel as if we had stepped into the pages of a beloved storybook.

As Jesus said in John 10:27, *"My children listen to my voice; I know them, and they follow me."* That's how we knew right away that our new friends, **Cherline, Nadia, Tyler, Jeremiah, Eliada, and Angel were also Christians**. We were all around the same age and shared so much in common. Like all Christian children, we believe in Jesus Christ as our Savior and Friend.

We learn to tell the truth, show kindness, forgive others, and keep our word. *"**Your word is a lamp to my feet and a light to my path.**"* Psalm 119:105. We sing the same worship songs, pray together, play, and celebrate special days like Christmas and Easter as one big family in Christ.

Dear Mommy and Daddy,

I want to sincerely thank you for taking us on such a wonderful trip to **Boston for Christmas in 2024**. It was truly one of the best Christmases ever, and we will always cherish the memories of it.

From the moment we landed at Logan Airport and stayed at the amazing InterContinental Hotel downtown, everything felt like a real Christmas movie. The snow, the

Christmas lights, the massive tree from Nova Scotia at **the Boston Common, and skating at the Frog Pond made it seem so magical.** Thank you for giving my brother and me warm gloves to share with Gershom, and for making sure we were all happy and comfortable, even when it was cold!

I loved watching **The Nutcracker at the Opera House**, as if it were a fairy tale come true. And I will never forget how much fun we had eating delicious food at **Faneuil Hall Marketplace** (Gershom's favorite!) and riding the **Polar Express** with our new friends from Jacksonville, Florida.

Your efforts have enabled us to create new memories every year, connect with other *Christian children who share our love for Jesus, and celebrate Christmas collectively as a family.* We appreciate your guidance in teaching us to love, share, and follow Jesus everywhere we go.

Even though it was cold, we loved cozy restaurants and even ice cream, just like you, Mommy! You always make every trip memorable with your love and laughter.

Thank you for everything you did to make this **Christmas truly special.** *I feel so blessed and proud to have you as my parents.* I love you so much, and I thank God for you every day.

Chapter Four

How Do You Talk to Jesus?

My Prayer and My Mind,
learning to pray

HEAVENLY CITIZEN

I Met Job and Learn About Talking to Jesus

Hello, my dear friend! Do you know a boy named Job? He was a student at my school last year, and he loves talking to Jesus. Every morning when he wakes up, he whispers a prayer. Before he eats his lunch, he thanks Jesus for his food. Even when he's walking home with his backpack full of books, he talks to Jesus in his heart like a best friend.

My name is Isaiah, and you already knew my little brother's name, "Gershom." We've discussed with Job about speaking to Jesus; at first, we thought it was by faith, yeah! Like believing in something to be true without seeing it.

Well, Job explained and asked us if we knew anything about **"The greatest commandment in the Law of God"**

My brother and I gave our answers and said, "To be saved and go to heaven or go to heaven forever." But Job said **"NO."** Then he explains:

He said that the answer was much bigger than that: every child must and should know the greatest law of the Lord,

"Love the Lord your God with all your heart and with all your soul and with all your mind." He said he prayed about everything in his heart; he is Jesus's best friend. (Matthew 22:37).

Job also enjoys **reading comic books**, and he's talented at drawing his characters. He and I were the only two Christian kids in our class, so we often shared stories about Jesus and prayed for each other. Job taught me that you can talk to Jesus anytime, anywhere, and He always listens! **"When God's children ask for help, Jesus hears and helps them every time."** (Psalm 34:17) Jesus lives in every child's heart.

Job taught us something very special: **Jesus loves it when you talk to Him in your heart!** Guess what? You

35

don't have to be grown-up, a teacher, or a pastor. You can be *the intelligent, kind person you are,* and Jesus will listen to every word you say. *"Glory to God in the highest heaven, and on earth peace to those on whom His favor rests."* (Luke 2:14)

When Jesus was twelve years old, He went to a festival with His parents, just as they always did. *"Everyone who heard Him speaking was amazed at His understanding and his answers about God's laws." (Luke 2:42-47)* Even as a boy, Jesus loved talking about God's words and telling the truth, just like my friend Job. And you can also speak to Him in your prayers.

> *What do you want to tell Jesus today*? Maybe you'd like to say, "Hi!" or *"Thank you for my family,"* or *"Please help me with my school test."* You can also ask him to heal you, or, if you know who is sick. Remember, *"Jesus is our healer, and He hears every prayer from every child's heart."* He'll be happy to hear from you anytime!

My friend Job shared this wonderful secret with me: Take a deep breath, smile, and say, "I am a child of God and a friend of Jesus." "We are wonderfully made in His image.

Then pray:

Hello, Jesus,

Thank you for loving me so much.

Thank you for making me smart and kind.

Thank you to my good friends and kind teachers.

Please bless my parents and all the children in the world.

I pray this in my friend Jesus' name, **Amen.**

Making New Friends for Jesus.

Esther is from the West Bank, specifically from Shiloh, a town in northern Jerusalem, Israel. She moved here when she was just a baby with her parents. Esther has long, beautiful hair and a gentle smile, but she is very shy and often keeps to herself. My brother and I decided to help her feel less lonely. We showed her how to pray silently in her heart and invited her to join us for lunch every day.

Over time, Esther opened up, and she became our friend. Now, Esther loves to laugh and share stories about her faith with us. She once told us that she has a best friend in her heart named Jesus. She says Jesus is the best friend anyone could have, because He never says, "I'm *too busy or I can't.*" He always listens with love. Can you think of something you want to tell Jesus right now? Whisper it or say it quietly in your heart; *He'll hear every word!*

Follow-up questions you could ask the children who are also friends with Jesus:

What did you tell Jesus in your heart just now?

How do you feel after talking to Him?

When do you like to talk to Jesus the most, in the morning, before bed, or when you're feeling happy or sad?

Do you have a special place where you enjoy praying?

What do you think Jesus says back to you when you talk to Him?

How can you help a shy friend, like *Isaiah and Gershom helped Esther?*

What's one thing you want to thank Jesus for today?

Do you know where Jerusalem is?

Do you know the meaning of your name?

Jesus is fair and kind.

He recognizes all the good things you do and how you show your love for Him by helping others. He will never forget how you continue to care for people. (Hebrews 6:10)

Gershom once shared this secret with me! I've tried it when I'm bored in class or in a place I don't like. He prayed quietly while sitting in class. When he couldn't speak out loud, he talked to Jesus silently in his mind. You can do this as well, anytime, anywhere! Jesus always listens.

When you help your friend with homework, you show Jesus' kindness.

When you share your games with your little brother, Gershom, you make Jesus smile.

When you forgive someone who has hurt you, you make Jesus proud!

Being kind and loving demonstrates that you are a genuine friend of Jesus. He enjoys seeing you care for others.

At home, you can help your parents without waiting to be asked. You can clean your room, pick up your toys, set the table for dinner, or wash the dishes.

You can be gentle with your baby brother or sister. You can share your favorite toy or read a book to them.

When you do these kinds of things, you show Jesus' love to your whole family! And guess what? Every kind word you speak and every kind action you take fill your home with joy and make everyone feel happier and closer together.

Jesus says:

"Be kind and compassionate to one another, forgiving each other, just as in Christ God forgave you." (Ephesians 4:32)

Remember, every time you choose kindness and forgiveness, you are shining Jesus' light in your family and to everyone you meet! *Because Christians are the light of the world.*

Jesus said we are the light of the world because **He wants us to shine with kindness, love, and goodness**, just like a bright light in a dark room helps people see. When we follow Him, **our words and actions can help others find the right way**, feel loved, and learn more about God. Being the light means showing the world what God's love looks like.

True or false: JESUS IS ALL ABOUT. THE TRUTH?

"You shall not say false things against other children or anyone." (Exodus 20:16). This means we must always tell

the truth and not lie about other people. When we speak the

truth, we make Jesus happy. When we lie, it makes Him sad.

Jesus teaches us that being honest is very important, *because*

He is the Truth Himself. In John 14:6, Jesus said, "*I am the way, the truth, and the life.*" So, when we tell the truth, we are walking in Jesus' way.

Jesus says, "The Lord detests lying lips, but he delights in people who are trustworthy" (Proverbs 12:22). This means

God disapproves of lying. But when we tell the truth, He is so pleased! In my family, we follow Jesus by telling the truth, even when it is hard. We know that Jesus already knows everything in our hearts, so it's better to be honest right away.

Instead, we should always tell the truth with love. Doing so helps us grow stronger in every way and become more like Christ, who is the head of the body. We learn that we should tell the truth with kindness and love. We do not share the truth to hurt someone but to help them. When we speak the truth this way, we grow closer to Jesus and become stronger, just like a tree grows healthier with water and sunlight.

The Bible tells us, "**Do not lie to each other**, since you have taken off your old self with Jesus practices." This means that when we belong to Jesus, we strive to live in a new, honest way. We don't want to be like **Ananias and Sapphira**. Ananias and his wife, Sapphira, sold a piece of property. They pretended to give all the money to the church, but instead, they kept part of the money for themselves. (Acts 5:3)

They lied and got into serious trouble because they didn't tell the truth. We can choose to be brave and honest, even if it's scary sometimes.

What would you do if you knew the truth that could get someone in trouble?

If you see something wrong and don't report it, someone might get hurt. We must learn to be honest and wise. Jesus wants children to think before they speak and not to talk too much, whether at school or at home. This is called wisdom, and it is a special gift from God. If we talk too much or lie, people will not believe us when we need them to.

When you are a friend of Jesus, you must tell Him and your parents the truth. You can trust them because they genuinely care about you and want to help. In my family, we always tell each other the truth. One day, my big brother **Gabe** told my parents that **Gershom** needed help with his math homework. **Gershom** was ashamed to ask and tried to hide it, because he knew that his two older brothers were very good at math. *Gabe knew the truth would help Gershom.*

Mommy and Daddy asked the big brothers to check his work and help him with his grades. Jesus said, "**A smart person doesn't talk too much and stays calm. Even someone who isn't wise can look smart if they stay quiet.**" When Daddy learned the truth, he took action immediately.

Instead of just helping Gershom with his other homework at the table, Daddy took him outside to the woods and a nearby river. *Daddy understood and discovered that Gershom was a visual learner*. He needed to see, touch, and feel things to understand them. Just as

Jesus knows each of us perfectly, Daddy knew precisely how to help Gershom.

What about you? *How do you learn best?* Are you a visual learner like **Gershom**, or do you prefer learning through *listening, reading, writing, or hands-on activities?* My big brother Gabe and I are **VARK** learners, which means we can grasp concepts easily regardless of the teaching approach.

What's your learning style?

Gershom is incredibly lucky! His dad was a teacher, his mom is brilliant, and his brothers are **VARK** learners, meaning they learn through various modalities, including pictures, listening, reading, writing, and hands-on activities. With such a family, learning is always enjoyable at Gershom's home!

If your family isn't available at home to support you with your schoolwork, don't worry, government programs offer tutors to help you in every school. Ask your teacher for assistance in signing up, so you can boost your grades. There's no shame in needing help! Unlike Gershom, who tried to hide his struggles, Jesus encourages us to seek the help we need, just as we offer support to others. Reaching out to teachers, friends, or siblings for help is both wise and positive.

After learning in nature with Daddy, Gershom's math was never a problem again. He started earning higher grades than everyone else in his class! Daddy helped make math come alive for him; he could smell the flowers, count the pebbles, and divide the sticks. As for me, Jesus has blessed me with the ability to learn quickly, so I now also assist my brother with his work. We have our after-school program, where we learn and grow together.

Telling the truth is a special skill that every child should learn. My brother and I trust each other's words because we know we always tell the truth.

What about you? Do you tell the truth to your parents and friends? Are you and your family friends with Jesus, too? Remember, when you tell the truth, you make Jesus happy and show that you are His special, brave, and honest friend.

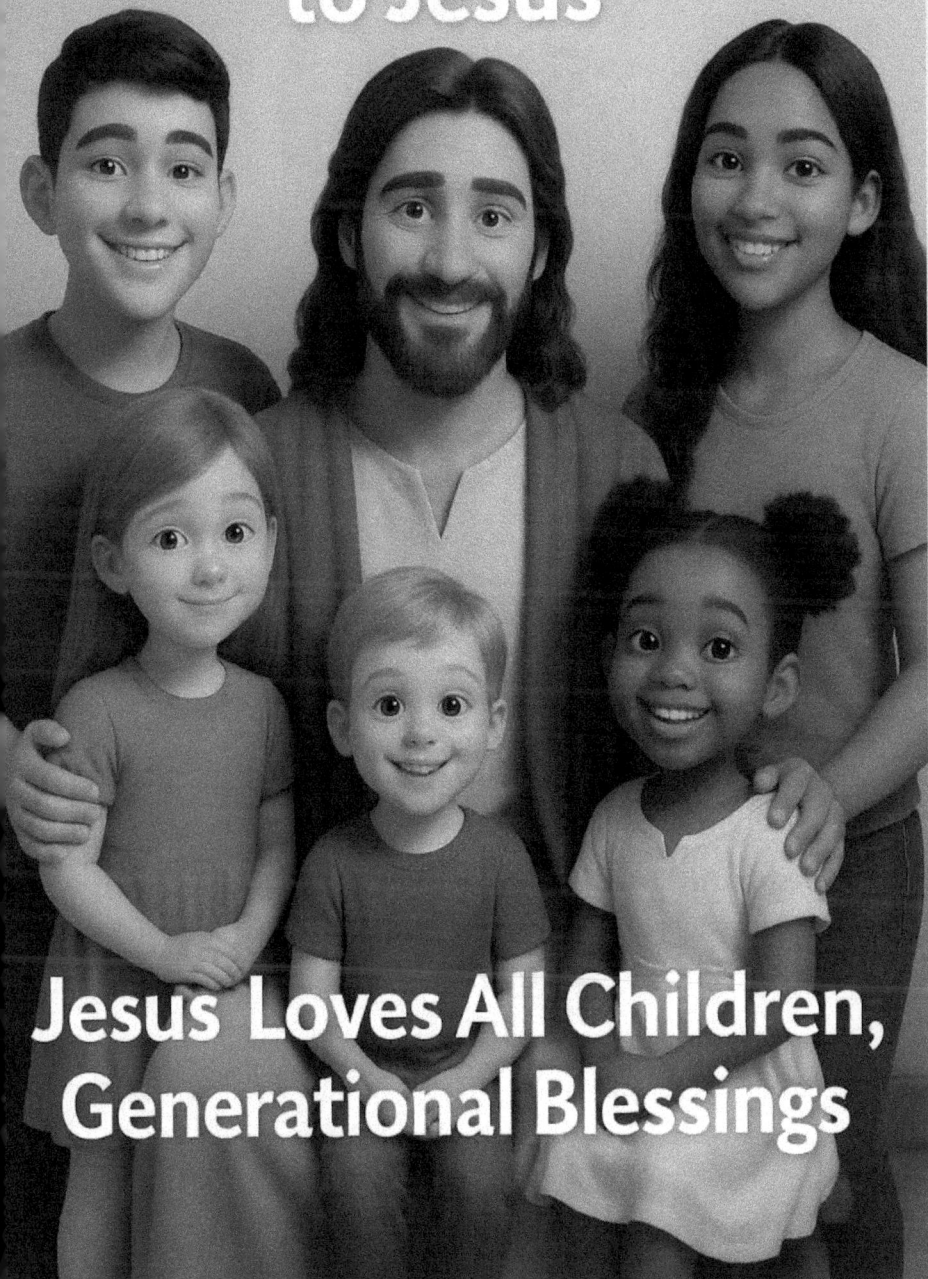

CHAPTER FIVE

My children belong to Jesus

Jesus Loves All Children, Generational Blessings

HEAVENLY CITIZEN

My children belong to Jesus.

Jesus Loves All Children

My children belong to Jesus.

Jesus Loves All Children

Jesus said: "Truly I tell you, anyone who will not receive the kingdom of God like a little child will never enter it."

(Luke 18:17)

There was a family that loved Jesus. They prayed together, laughed together, traveled together, and supported each other. Every day, they talked about how special Jesus was to them and how He was their friend.

Then people brought little children to Jesus so He could place His hands on them and pray. Jesus said, **"Whosoever shall receive one of such children in my name, receiveth me: and whosoever shall receive me, receiveth not me, but him that sent me."** After He placed His hands on them, He moved on from there. And He blessed all the children." (**Mark 9:37**)

Jesus called all children, boys and girls, His friends, and He said they **all belong to the Kingdom of Heaven**. One day, all children will see Jesus in person in Heaven, but for now, we must pray every day, do good things for one another, and be kind to everyone, regardless of their origin.

If you welcome and care for a child as you would for me, it's like you are welcoming me."(Matthew 18:5)

When we show kindness to other children, Jesus blesses us in wonderful ways. **He helps us excel in school, earn good grades, and achieve our dreams.** Plus, Jesus sends special messages to our parents. That's why my parents pray every day, asking Jesus for His blessings and protection for us.

Jesus teaches children to do good to others, regardless of who they are or where they come from.

Every Christian child is part of the Kingdom of Heaven. Even as a child, Jesus was brilliant. He was wise, gentle, respectful, and deeply loving towards others. He often spoke of His Father in heaven, showing reverence and devotion while also honoring His earthly parents.

His desire was for the entire world to grow in love and kindness toward each other. At the same time, He wanted us to seek knowledge and understanding of God's Kingdom so that we could live with wisdom, compassion, and truth.

If you're good at math and a friend excels at science, we can support each other and build a strong friendship! Every child has an angel in heaven watching over them. My angel observes everything I do. That's why my family feels blessed, because we follow Jesus' teachings to show kindness to everyone.

Remember to treat *all children with kindness and respect*. They are like angels and constantly have a special connection with Heaven. Let's value and safeguard the gentle innocence and happiness.

Generational blessings

Many years ago, in the beautiful country of **Israel**, a king named David made a significant change to the country's capital. **He renamed the capital from Hebron to Jerusalem.** His son became king after him. King Solomon built a magnificent temple in this city, where the

Ark of the Covenant, a sacred gold-covered chest, was kept. This was a divine secret, entrusted by God to His faithful servants, such as **King David and King Solomon.** They are father and son. Additionally, the grandson of King Solomon, Rehoboam, succeeded his father as king.

What happens if you don't listen to your parents
Or grandparents?

Let's look at the kings of Israel. **King David** was brave and faithful, bringing all of God's people together as one strong family. His son, *King Solomon*, was very wise and wealthy, and he built the Temple of God; however, he later made wrong choices that turned his heart away from God.

Solomon's son, **King Rehoboam, didn't listen to wise advice from his dad,** and because of that, the kingdom broke into two parts, and the people didn't live happily together anymore. This is why your parents remind you to behave well, be kind to everyone, be respectful, and be thankful, because wise choices help keep families and friendships strong.

Children should show respect for their parents.

There was a man named Paul, also known as the **Apostle Paul.** He was a writer and teacher who gently reminded us that *children should obey their parents in everything.* This means listening carefully and doing what our parents ask us to do, helping us grow and learn together.

God gave our parents a very special responsibility: to guide, teach, and care for us. When we obey our parents, we show that we trust God's plan for our family. Part of that plan is respecting the wisdom and care that God has given to our parents.

Obeying our parents isn't just about following rules; it's about building trust and love within our family. This is what Apostle Paul wrote in the Bible in Colossians 3:20. *"Children, always listen to your parents and do what they ask you to do. This pleases God."*

Obedience as an Expression of Love for God and
my parents

When kids obey their parents, it's not just about following rules or avoiding trouble. It's actually about obeying God! Jesus tells children to respect and honor their parents because when they do, they are following God's plan for their lives.

In Ephesians 6:1-3, the Bible promises that when you obey your parents, things will go well for you, and you will have a long, happy life on Earth. *Jesus will ensure you live longer here.*

So, when you listen to your parents, you not only make them happy but also show love and respect to God, who gave your parents the critical responsibility of caring for you. Your parents will be very proud of you.

My parents are Jesus' representatives in our home, and they are responsible for caring for me and all the children in our family. *When I obey them, I show respect and love for them.* Without my parents providing me with a place to sleep, a safe home to return to after school, food to eat, and a space to play, I would be in a difficult situation. For all these things, I am thankful and love my mommy and daddy for their hard work in taking care of me. From now on, *I vow to listen to and obey my parents, and to tell them how much I appreciate and love them.*

Obedience in God's Family

Obedience to parents constitutes one of the initial and most critical lessons acquired during childhood. As individuals mature, they will encounter circumstances requiring decision-making and confronting challenges. At this juncture, parental support becomes most essential. Cultivating the practice of obedience and respect towards our parents in all matters establishes a fundamental basis for making prudent choices and respecting authority throughout one's life.

Furthermore, *my family was the first place where I experienced God's love and learned important lessons from my parents*. The teachings of Jesus guide me to respect my parents and follow God's Word. Because of this, obeying my parents becomes a meaningful part of my lifelong journey to follow God's will, bringing me fulfillment and peace.

King Solomon said in Proverbs 1:8-9: "Listen, my son, to your father's instruction and do not forsake your mother's teaching. They are a garland to grace your head and a chain to adorn your neck." This means that when you listen to the wise advice your parents give you, it's like putting on a beautiful crown and a shiny necklace. Just as a crown makes you look special, following your parents' teachings makes your heart and life lovely.

Their wisdom helps you make informed choices, stay safe, and develop into a kind and intelligent person. You will have Jesus' grace in your life to help you excel in school as well. So, every time you listen and learn from your parents, it's like wearing something that makes you shine, feel good, and look beautiful.

"Do you know why Jesus loves children so much?" Mommy asked as she sat with Gershom on the couch. "Why?" said little brother Gershom, with his eyes wide open with curiosity. "Because children are special to Jesus. He loves how pure and trusting you are. He wants you to be close to Him, like we want to be close to each other." Mommy smiled gently. "Jesus is the only person in the whole world who can see into every child's heart and mind to know how good we are." We love everyone; we do good to each other, right, mommy?"

Gershom nodded, feeling the warmth of her words. "That's right, my baby boy," she said. Children, obey your parents in the Lord, for this is right. (Ephesians 6:1) Including you, Gershom, and your brothers, Gabe and Isaiah.

Daddy, on the other hand, is the family's teacher; he taught us something just as important. He said, "When we're sad or feeling sick, we need to share our thoughts with our family," he would say. "That way, we can pray together to ask Jesus for good health and comfort." Mommy agreed, adding, "In any good family, there are no secrets. We need to be open like a book with lots and lots of stories so that we can help each other." Gershom smiled, thinking about the love and care that surrounded him, both from his family and from Jesus.

Grandpa is also the most fun person to be around. He constantly invents new games for us to play, keeping us entertained and making us laugh along the way. He has some fantastic stories about when Mommy was little. He told us that once, Mommy was very sick, and Grandpa prayed to **Jesus** for her to get better. And guess what? Jesus heard his prayers and healed Mommy!

We all feel so blessed in our family. Our hearts are filled with love for each other, and Grandpa reminds us every day that the most important thing is to trust and follow Jesus, just as our family does.

My grandma *Anna* loves giving big hugs! We enjoy her cooking, and she always surprises us with little gifts. She has so much love for us, and we pray that Jesus keeps her healthy and happy for many years to come.

Our other grandma, *Consessa*, is a **prayer warrior for our family.** She says, "***My prayers will protect you, my children, and your children, for many generations.***"

Both of our grandmas are Christians, and we feel very blessed because of that.

How about you? Do you still have grandparents with you?

Take a moment to thank them and express your love. If they are no longer here, let's pray that Jesus brings you comfort and happiness with your family.

My Grandma Anna
Grandma Anna gives hugs so tight,
Her cooking fills our hearts with joy. She brings us gifts, a sweet surprise. We pray for her with joyful eyes.

My Grandma Consessa prays every day, covering us with love.

Her prayers protect us, near and far, like shining lights, like a bright star, the prayer warrior for our family.
We feel so lucky to know you; blessings are with you!

Our Blessing
Both our grandmas love Jesus, true. We're so blessed because of you!
Do you have grandparents, too?
Thank them now for all they do.

If they're gone, don't feel sad,
Jesus loves you, makes hearts glad.
With family near, or far apart,
His love will fill your heart with happiness.

Chapter Six

Do you have a humble spirit?

Do you have a loving heart for others?

HEAVENLY CITIZEN

Do you have a humble spirit?

To be close to Jesus, children don't need to be the smartest, fastest, or loudest. Jesus smiles when he sees a humble heart, someone who knows they need help, who asks questions, and who wants to learn. Jesus said, "Therefore, *whoever humbles himself like this little child is the greatest in the kingdom of heaven.*" (Matthew 18:4)

This means that the greatest in God's eyes are not the proud, but the humble children. A gentle child says, "*I need Jesus.*" He is kind to others, patient in learning, and willing to say "*I'm sorry*" when he makes a mistake. Jesus sees your kind heart and says, "*This is my friend.*"

Jesus' friends listen to His words and lovingly try to follow them. Jesus said, "*You are my friends if you do everything I ask you to do*" (John 15:14). Obeying Jesus doesn't mean we have to be perfect, but that we try to do what is right, because we love Him. This can mean *being honest, even when it hurts, being kind, even when it's hard, and helping others, even when it's difficult.*

This can also mean *being honest even when it is tough, helping a sad friend, or choosing to share something we'd rather keep to ourselves.* Every time a child decides kindness over sadness, truth over lies, and love over selfishness, they become best friends with Jesus. Obedience is a sign of love, and Jesus notices every small act of kindness.

That is why you are his faithful friend.

Do you have a loving heart for others?

Jesus is a genuine friend to those who show love to others. He said, "*Love one another. As I have loved you, so you must love one another*" (John 13:34). When a child forgives someone who has hurt them, shares with a brother or sister, or comforts someone sad, they are showing the heart of Jesus.

Loving others is one of *the most powerful ways to demonstrate that you are a friend of Jesus*. He doesn't just want us to love Him; He wants us to treat others as He treats us: with patience, kindness, and forgiveness. A child who carries love in the heart is a child who walks closely with Jesus.

Talking to Jesus in prayer,

Being Jesus' friend means talking to him every day. That's what prayer is: talking to Jesus as you would speak to your best friend. The Gospel says, "Pray without stopping" (1 Thessalonians 5:17), which means we can talk to Jesus at any time, anywhere. Whether you are happy, sad, scared, or thankful, Jesus is always ready to listen to you. You don't need to use complicated words or know special prayers; speak from your heart. Just like Peter's prayer in our story, a sincere and straightforward prayer brings joy to Jesus. He listens carefully to every word spoken by a child and keeps every prayer close to his heart.

Accept Jesus into your heart.

The best part about being Jesus' friend is that *you don't have to earn it or prove yourself; it's a gift*. Jesus offers His friendship as a *gift*. Jesus says, "**You love because I first loved you**" (1 John 4:19). This means Jesus loved you even before you knew His name. You don't need to be perfect, wealthy, or essential to be His friend.

All you have to do is accept His love. Accepting Jesus' love means opening your heart and allowing Him to be a part of you. When a child says, "Jesus, *I love you*," He responds, "*I have always loved you before you were born*." That's the kind of friend Jesus is: loving, faithful, and eternal. Because of your friendship with Him, *you are now a child of His Heavenly Kingdom*.

Prayer

Hello, Jesus, my Friend.

My name is Gabe, and my little brothers are Isaiah and Gershom.

We thank You for our family and for all of our friends. Please bless every child who is reading this book.

Now, we are all your new friends, and we pray that you will stay close to us. Protect us, guide us, and fill our hearts with Your love.

In Your holy name we pray, Amen.

The Secret Connection Between Us

Do you have a humble spirit? Do you possess a heart that loves others?

One of the best ways to develop that kind of heart is to spend time talking to Jesus in prayer and inviting Him to live in your heart.

Have you ever traveled to another town with your parents, to school, or maybe to visit a close family member?

Sometimes, on these trips, you meet other children who are so kind and friendly. You smile at them, and they smile back. You play together, share a snack, or laugh at something silly, and it feels like you've known each other forever.

Why is that?

It's because we are all children of the same Creator, connected in ways we can't always see. Even if you meet someone who doesn't speak your language, you can still find ways to communicate: a wave, a gesture, a shared game. When we do this, we practice humility and choose kindness, even with strangers.

Sometimes, it's funny how quickly we develop feelings for someone. You might think, *"I like this person... but wait, I don't even know their name yet!"* That's part of the beautiful design God created in our world.

Look at nature, every creature of the same kind has a special bond. Fish of the same species swim together. Lions, though fierce to other animals, are gentle with their pride. Peregrine falcons are known as the fastest animals on Earth when diving for prey, reaching speeds of over 240 miles per hour (386 kilometers per hour). But even they share a connection with others of their kind. When they are scared or flying through a storm, they might soar even faster, sometimes exceeding 400 kilometers per hour, yet they stay calm when flying with their fellow falcons.

It's all by design.

We humans are meant to share a special bond. We're built to care for, help, and protect one another. But sometimes, we forget. Life gets busy, challenges arise, and we may focus only on ourselves. Christian children generally do not refer to someone as selfish because they understand that such individuals will find ways to assist those they care about. Therefore, we might say, "**You are slow to assist others.**"

Then, something happens that reminds us of our interconnectedness. Imagine you're on an airplane, and it suddenly hits turbulence. Or you're in a car that begins sliding on an icy road. In moments like those, whether someone is a Christian or not, almost everyone finds themselves calling out to God for help. The heart naturally reaches upward when afraid, just as it naturally reaches outward toward others in kindness when things are calm.

That's because deep down, *we all know we are not alone. We're part of something bigger*, a family that spans towns, countries, and even languages. When we live humbly, we're living the way we were created to live.

Humbleness doesn't mean thinking less of yourself. It means remembering that others matter just as much as you do. *It's letting someone go first in line*, sharing your toys, or helping someone pick up their dropped books. It's listening before speaking and trying to understand before judging.

Choosing a humble life makes your heart kinder, more loving, and open to connecting with others, even strangers. *Those connections can develop into lifelong friendships.*

So, the next time you meet someone new, remember: it's not a coincidence. You might not speak the same language. You might not be from the same place. But you are connected, just like the lions, the fish, and the falcons. And that connection is a gift, one you can honor by showing kindness, humility, and love.

Because in the end, no matter where we come from, *we're all part of one great, beautiful design.*

Chapter Seven

My dad is a 68W, a soldier who heals

Daddy will be home for Christmas

HEAVENLY CITIZEN

A Hero in Uniform, a Servant of Christ,
and a Daddy with a Big Heart

Dad is a medic in the United States Army! *His name is David*, just like King David in the Bible. He is trained to assist soldiers who are injured during battles. He provides first aid, stops bleeding, and saves lives right on the battlefield. My dad is also a hero, not just because of his uniform, *but because he always helps people, no matter who they are, what they look like, or where they come from.*

Daddy says he is a soldier in Christ. He reads his Bible and prays every day, and he taught me Psalm 144:1: *"God makes my heart strong and my hands ready to do good things."* Daddy says this means God gives him strength and courage to do his job. Even when he is far away, he tells me God is always with him.

Sometimes my daddy goes on a peacekeeping mission **for the United Nations (UN).** He travels to different countries where there are problems, and he helps children and families who are hurt or scared. Even if they speak a different language, Daddy gives them medicine, food, and comfort. He says being a medic means helping everyone, even if they used to be enemies.

One day, I asked Daddy why he didn't just work in a hospital instead. He smiled and said, *"Gershom, I'm a Christian who wants to make a difference in the world. There will always be wars, whether I go or not, but if I go, I can help many people who don't have the money to pay for healthcare. I'm not a soldier to fight. I'm a soldier to care for God's children."* And I knew, right then, my daddy truly has a big heart, and I want to be just like him. He is my hero. I thank you, Jesus, for blessing me with a great dad.

My mom is a hilarious person. She always finds ways to make me laugh, even when I feel sad or sick. Her silly faces, dancing in the kitchen, and bedtime jokes make everything better. Jesus says in Proverbs 17:22, **"A**

cheerful heart is good medicine," and I think God gave my mom a heart full of joy to help heal ours with laughter.

Mommy's faith in Jesus is strong. We call her **the prayer warrior in our family** because she prays for everyone, all the time. She prays for Daddy when he's away, for us kids, for her friends, and even for people she doesn't know. **1 Thessalonians 5:17** says, *"Pray without ceasing,"* and that's just what Mommy does; she talks to Jesus all day long, and it makes her strong and full of peace.

What's even funnier is how Mommy prays out loud, so loudly that everyone in the house knows exactly what she's saying to Jesus! She always starts by singing her favorite worship songs. Then, with a big smile, she begins talking out loud, as if Jesus is sitting right beside her at the kitchen table.

"How are you doing today, Jesus?" she says.

"It's a good day to be alive. Well, I'm so glad to be here with my whole family, safe and healthy."

Then she continues to pray, thanking Jesus for everything, especially for us. She says, *"Hey, Jesus, we know you are so good! Our safety, and the safety of the whole world, is in Your hands."* **Then she adds,** *"Jesus, bless them forever, and bless every child everywhere.* Amen!

Every mommy's prayers are filled with love, joy, and thanksgiving, just as Jesus states in Philippians 4:6: **"Do not be anxious about anything, but in every situation, by** *prayer and petition, with thanksgiving, present your requests to God."*

My little brother, Gershom, and I know our mom's prayer so well that we can recite it ourselves!

When Mommy reaches the end, we always jump in together and say, *"Bless them today and forever, and* bless every child everywhere. Amen!" It makes us all laugh and feel close, like we're part of one big prayer team for our family.

Talking to Jesus as you would to a best friend can bring comfort during times of loneliness and isolation. Prayer doesn't need to be elaborate or filled with big words; it simply needs to come from your heart genuinely. In our home, her prayers are joyful and full of love, often accompanied by the little voices of her children saying "Amen" together.

Even when Daddy is far away, they pray and talk to each other every day. Thanks to technology, Mommy and Daddy can see each other on video or make calls from across the world. We all get to join in and see Daddy, too! Sometimes, he even shows us the people he's helping overseas. Mommy smiles big when she sees him, and then we all hold hands and pray together.

Matthew 18:20 Jesus says: "For where two or three gather in my name, there am I with them." Even if we're far apart, God is with us!

I feel so blessed to have a mommy like her. She is joyful, faithful, and full of love. When I look at her, I see the love of Jesus shining through.

Thank you, Mommy, for making our home bright with laughter, strong with prayer, and warm with love. I love you so much, more than all the stars in the sky!

Daddy Will Be Home for Christmas

Now it's the end of November, and every year, there's exciting news in our house: *Daddy will be coming home for Christmas!* We've circled the date on the *kitchen calendar* in big red letters and added shiny gold stars around it. In the house, I have a special map that shows precisely where Daddy is. Next to it, I also keep my countdown calendar, and every day I mark off one more square.

Just a few more days to go!

Daddy is working far away in a place called the **Gaza Strip**, a land near the **eastern Mediterranean Sea**, bordered by **Israel**, **Egypt**, and the Mediterranean Sea. This land is rich in history and has many stories to tell, making it a place full of character, charm, and sadness. But Daddy is there doing **humanitarian work with the UN**, helping people who are sick or hurt, especially children and families. He always tells me, *"Jesus sends us to where love and care are needed most."*

The Bible mentions Gaza! In Acts 8:26-28, it says: "Now an angel of the Lord said to Philip, *'Go south to the road, a desert road that goes down from Jerusalem to Gaza.'*" On that road, Philip met an essential Ethiopian official who was reading the Book of Isaiah. Philip explained the prophecy about Jesus to him, and the man believed and was baptized. *He became a friend of Jesus on the road.* That same road is where my Daddy is working now, **walking in the *footsteps of love and service, led by the Holy Spirit, just like Philip.***

Now it's almost time for him to come home. My heart feels like it's full of butterflies, and I can't stop smiling. Every morning, I say, "*One day closer!*" I'm working on a special welcome gift for Daddy, a card with drawings and a poem.

It's a secret; no one knows about it. I tell Jesus in my prayers everything I want to share with Him. Mommy, Gabe, and Gershom are preparing the house, and we're counting down the minutes! He'll fly home on *a big Air Force military plane, wearing his uniform*, and when I see him, I'll run as fast as I can and hug my hero. This will be the best Christmas ever, because our family will be together again.

Hello, New Friend

Hi there! I'm so glad to read with you. My name is *Isaiah*, and I want to share a little about my family.

I live with my mommy and daddy, and I can tell you something special about them: **they are friends with Jesus. Yes, they are real friends!** They talk to Him every day in prayer. My mom is what we call a **prayer warrior for our family**; she prays out loud and sings to Jesus with such joy that it fills the whole house with light.

My dad is in the army; he's a medic who cares for everyone in need. Even when he's far away helping people, he never forgets to pray. He always reminds me, "**Jesus is with us, even when we're far apart.**"

My brother's names are Gabe and Gershom. **We are best friends in the whole wide world.** We play, laugh, and sometimes even pray together. And guess what? We talk about Jesus as if He were present here in the room, because we believe He is always with us in our hearts. He has our angels with us wherever we go for protection.

Now, let me ask you something:

Do you want to be a friend of Jesus, too? It's the best friendship in the world. You don't need to be perfect. You don't have to see Him with your eyes; you have to believe in your heart. Hebrews 11:1 "**Faith means trusting God, even when we can't see what He's doing. We believe He is working and will keep His promises.**"

My daddy once told me, "**When you close your eyes, you can see Jesus in your mind. No distractions. Just you and Him.**" You can talk to Jesus anytime, out loud, quietly, or just in your heart. And when you do, He listens.

Let's Pray Together

So now, my new friend, will you pray with me?

Close your eyes briefly. Take a deep breath. Picture Jesus standing beside you, smiling. He's listening.

Here is my prayer for **you:**

Lord Jesus,

Our Father in heaven,

Hallowed be your name.

Let your kingdom come, and your will be done in the lives of my new friends who are reading this book.

I ask that you bless them, heal them, and love their families deeply.

Show them that you are genuine and genuinely care about every aspect of their lives.

Bless their mommies and daddies. Bless their brothers, sisters, and friends.

Help them excel in school and provide them with joyful, peaceful homes.

Make them intelligent, kind, and full of your love. Lord Jesus, receive them today as your new friends. We love you. Thank you for loving us first.

In Your holy and beautiful name, I pray. **Amen.**

Chapter Eight

Welcome to God's Family, My Friends

Many Hero Mothers from Afar: Christian Moms

HEAVENLY CITIZEN

Welcome to God's Family, My Friend!

From now on, remember that you are a beloved child of God. You are dearly loved, chosen, and beautifully made by God. *This means you are a precious citizen of the kingdom of heaven.*

One of the most fabulous kings of God was David. He was a musician who touched the Lord's heart with his songs. In Psalm 139:14, he said: *"I praise You because I am fearfully and wonderfully made; Your works are wonderful; I know that full well." That I am perfect just the way you made me.*

That means God created you with great care and love. You are not an accident; you are God's masterpiece, intentionally designed for a special purpose! Jesus knows your name, and He says you belong to Him. He holds you safely in His right hands, and nothing can take you away from His love.

Romans 8:39 "Nothing in the whole world can ever separate my children from my love, because they belong to me!"

Here's a simple truth you can keep in mind every day:

God made you special, Jesus loves you always,

You are His child, and you belong to Him forever!

Jesus loves you, and you are part of his kingdom.

Welcome to God's family!

Many Hero Mothers from Afar: Christian Moms
A Special Mission

Our Hero Moms, the Military Mothers

Our government does something good and kind, something that makes Jesus happy, when it helps other countries abroad. The government sends our military and army far out of our country to help people in need.

Sometimes they travelled to countries that are part of the North Atlantic Treaty Organization (NATO). NATO is an alliance of countries in North America and Europe that was formed in 1949 to provide collective security among its members. They also deployed to other countries like Israel, Ukraine, Egypt, Jordan, Afghanistan, and Pakistan. Many mothers serve in the military to help other mothers and children, providing healthcare, food, and comfort, just as Gershom's father did long ago." Mr. Moise'

Do you know any mothers who are serving in the military?

Josh's mother has a very special job. She wears a uniform and helps protect people worldwide. Sometimes she has to travel far to work in another country. When she leaves, her family feels a little sad. But she always reassures them that her job is to help keep everyone safe and bring peace wherever she goes.

I am very proud to recognize that many brave women, like Josh's mother, are heroes who have a significant impact on the world. *"Be strong and courageous. Do not be afraid or discouraged, for the Lord your God is with you wherever you go."* (Joshua 1:9)

Josh is Gabe's best friend from school, and they've been friends since kindergarten.

Did you know that there were courageous Christian women in the Bible who were also Heroes?

Many mothers today serve with honor in top ranks across the world's armies, and we are proud of their courage and dedication. Their strength, discipline, and sacrifice remind us that service is not limited by gender but is a calling that requires bravery and commitment. Yet above all human skill and training, we entrust them to God's protection, asking Him to shield them in every battle, guide their steps, and bring them home safely to the families who love and await them.

Yes, there was a brave woman named. *Deborah*. She was a prophetess and a judge in Israel (Judges 4-5). Deborah didn't carry a sword, but she led an army and helped her people win because she trusted Jesus with all her heart! There was also *Miriam*, who led the women in singing and dancing after God saved them from danger at the Red Sea (Exodus 15). She didn't fight in a battle, but she helped everyone praise God with joy and courage.

Like Deborah and Miriam, Josh's mother is a heroic woman who loves Jesus and helps others wherever she goes.

Counting the Days

When our moms are not around, we feel their absence instantly. Some mothers are in the military, some are on business trips, and others go to work daily.

However, we have a special way to stay close to them: we use a calendar specifically designed for their trips.

One morning at school, my friend Rosa showed me her calendar. She added a new sticker because her mom is also traveling with the army. When the calendar is full of colorful stickers, it means her mom will be coming home soon!

Sometimes it feels like forever, but each sticker reminds us that we are one day closer to that big, warm hug. It's the same thing my brothers Isaiah, Gershom, and I did when our dad was gone. Thanks to Jesus, he's now home!

I also drew pictures for him and wrote him letters. Sometimes I sketched hearts, medical helicopters, or even him in his uniform. He loved receiving my letters because they made him feel close to me, even when we were far apart.

Talking from Afar

This part is challenging for all families. Even though our mothers are far away, we always find ways to stay in touch with them. We call them on the phone, send messages, and sometimes do video calls. When I see my friends Rosa and Josh looking at their mother's face on the screen, their hearts warm, and they are filled with happiness.

Sometimes, she shows them photos of her workplace and her new friends, just like Dad used to do. My friends and I love listening to military stories.

The Big Hugs

Finally, the most exciting day arrives, the day my friends' moms come home!

My friends run as fast as they can and throw themselves into their moms' arms, giving the biggest hugs ever! They tell them all about the stickers, drawings, and all the fun things they did while they were away.

The moms smile and hold them close. I understand that feeling, which I experienced when my dad was away. Even when they're far, we pray for them every day, asking Jesus to keep them safe from harm.

Do you know any hero parents working abroad as well?

Perhaps you can share their stories and express gratitude to God for their courage and love.

Prayer for our heroic mothers

Dear Jesus,

` Thank you, Jesus, for giving us courageous mothers who serve and help people everywhere. They wear special uniforms and carry out essential duties to ensure the safety of others and provide them with peace of mind.

Sometimes they travel great distances to countries like Israel, Ukraine, Jordan, or even Afghanistan.

Even though we miss them a lot, we know they show their love through every kind gesture they make. Stay near our mothers when they are away.

Help them feel our hugs, letters, and love, even from afar.

Protect them always and ensure they return home happy and strong. We are very proud of them, just like Deborah and Miriam in the Bible, because they are strong, kind, and full of courage.

Help us be patient as we wait, and remind us daily that You are always with them and with us, too. We thank you for Rosa's mom, Josh's mom, and all the mothers who help others around the world.

Bless all the heroic moms today, and let them know how much we love them. In Your power, we pray, **Amen.**

Chapter Nine
You are a good kid:
Learning to Listen Like Jesus

The wise Christian children need to listen

HEAVENLY CITIZEN

The wise children need to learn to listen.

"*Smart children listen to their parents, but a rude child ignores correction.*" **King Solomon** means that when you're a wise child, you pay attention to what your parents and teachers say, because they're trying to help you grow more intelligent.

Taming the Wild Heart: Learning to Listen Like Jesus. How Wise Kids Become Strong Through Loving Obedience.

Proverbs 13:1:

"A smart child listens to their parents, but a rude child ignores correction."

There's a boy at my school named **Samuel**. He talks a lot, especially during school trips when we're supposed to listen. He doesn't think that getting good grades matters. He once said, "It's only to make parents happy!" But our teacher, **Ms. Hannah**, says, **"Without good grades and good behavior, no one moves up to the next class."**

Even though his mother encourages him to finish his homework, **Samuel** prefers playing video games. He stays up late to play, and when he gets to class, he either falls asleep or talks back to anyone trying to help him. **Ms. Hannah** had to call his mom, and she had to leave her job, just to come to school and talk with him. That day, **Samuel** looked sad, but it wasn't because he felt sorry for himself. He didn't want his mom to be upset. **Why do you think that is?** That means Samuel loves his mom, and he will do better to keep her happy.

That's the kind of love Jesus wants.

When I saw that, I thought about how much my parents love me and my little brothers. If it had been one of us, we'd be in big trouble. Papa doesn't mess around when it comes to discipline and self-respect. He would take away our games (we don't have any games at the house, my dad says "games are the biggest distractions for a student"), make us write a letter of apology to the teachers, and most importantly, ensure we understood why we needed to change.

Isaiah and Gershom work hard to keep their grades up, not just to avoid trouble, but to make our family proud. Mama always says, "**When you learn well, you shine bright.**" Papa says, "**God is pleased when children listen.**" So, we do our best. We might not always earn perfect scores, but we put in our best effort. Jesus will be happy, because it's also for our future; that's what Daddy said.

One day, **Samuel** saw my test score and said, "**You always get good grades. Your parents must give you everything.**" I smiled and replied, "**Nope**". They give me love and rules. I listen to them, and that helps me do well." He didn't answer, but I saw him thinking. Maybe he is starting to understand.

So, if you want to be a **wise kid like Gershom**, remember this: listen to the people God has placed in your home to guide you, including your parents, teachers, and elders. They're not just giving rules to be mean; they're guiding you, because they love you. Just as God corrects those He loves, our parents help shape our lives into the children God created us to be.

Remember: **A bright child listens.** A rude child ignores. **Choose wisdom,** and watch how Jesus blesses your learning to make you intelligent.

All Christian children, boys and girls, are exceptional and bright because they pray. Prayer makes us strong and wise.

In the Bible, James 1:5 says:

"If any of you lacks wisdom, let him ask of God, who gives to all generously and without reproach, and it will be given to him."

We learn to pray from our parents, who teach us to communicate with God and trust in Jesus every day. When we pray, we open our hearts and let Jesus fill our hearts with love and light.

Jesus is the greatest friend anyone could ever have! He is not selfish, hypocritical, or jealous. In John 15:15, Jesus says, *"I have called you friends, for everything that I learned from my Father I have made known to you."* Jesus wants to be our closest friend; someone we can always trust and rely on to keep our secrets. When we feel lonely or scared, we can talk to Him at any time, and He will always listen to make things better.

When Jesus was a boy, He loved all the children around Him. He played with them, shared stories, and taught them about God's love. Two of His best friends were His little brothers, James and Jude. Jesus taught them how to respect one another and be kind to everyone. He was never mean or rude. Instead, He was gentle and caring, showing us how to live like true children of God. Then he said, "**The kingdom of My father in heaven belongs to you**".

Jesus also took care of His little sisters. As an older brother, He protected them and helped them learn about God's truth. Ephesians 4:32 says, "**Be kind to one another, tenderhearted, forgiving one another, as God in Christ forgave you.**" Jesus showed His sisters how to be kind and brave. Because Jesus was so friendly and helpful, everyone loved being around Him, and His job as a big brother was joyful and easy.

Jesus taught His brothers and sisters that no one is better, more beautiful, or more intelligent than anyone else. He told them that we are all made in the image of God. Genesis 1:27 says, "*So God created all of us in His image; in the image of God, He created him; boys and girls, He created them.*" Jesus wanted them to know they were perfectly made, handsome, and beautiful just as they were.

Now, you are a child of God as well. If you take a look in a mirror, is there anything missing? I know you were wonderfully made in the image of God, just the way you are. You don't need anyone else to tell you because Jesus tells you:

"**You're beautiful just the way you are.**" **Jesus also told them not to listen to anyone who claimed they were not good enough.**

When other children tried to bully His **brothers and sisters**, they could not succeed. Their confidence was *too strong* because they knew Jesus was always with them. Isaiah 41:10 reminds us, "**Don't be afraid, because I am with you. Don't worry, because I am your God. I will make you strong, help you, and hold you safe in my hands.**"

Now that you are a Christian, *you are part of Jesus' big family plan!* You are like one of His little brothers or sisters. When you look in the mirror, you can say, "My name is Gershom, Gabe, Isaiah, Job, Angie, Josh, or add your name here ----------------. *God beautifully makes us.*

The Lord Jesus Christ is our best friend. "I look good just the way *I am*". I don't need makeup or extra things, *because God made me perfectly as I am.* Psalm 139:14 says, "*I praise you because I am fearfully and wonderfully made, I thank you, O my Lord and savior.*"

Jesus says to you, "*I am watching over you and I will never leave your side nor forsake you. You are my child.*" When you pray and sing to Jesus, He listens with a big smile. So, always remember that *you are special, you are loved, and you belong to God's beautiful family forever!*

Now, as a child of God, you need to learn how to pray. Prayer is a special way of talking with Jesus. It's like having a secret telephone number to speak directly to Jesus, only to Him! In 1 Thessalonians 5:17, the Bible instructs us to *"Pray without ceasing."* This means we can talk to Jesus at any time and from anywhere. When you pray, you are sharing your heart with Him, and He is always listening.

Jesus says, '**Call to me, and I will answer you. I will tell you wonderful things you don't know yet.**' (Jeremiah 33:3)

When you become a Christian, you gain a very special friend, Jesus! However, this friendship differs from the ones you have at school, church, or in your neighborhood. It is a personal friendship, meaning it's one-of-a-kind just between you and Jesus. In the Bible, John 15:14, Jesus says, "**You are my friends if you do what I tell you.**" Jesus wants to be your closest friend, the one who understands you better than anyone else ever could.

Jesus said: **We should love Him with all our heart, soul, and mind.** *In Matthew 22:37, Jesus doesn't want children to miss out on the greatest commandment to be part of God's kingdom. This is why he made sure all children learn how to love the Lord; he tells a group of his friends to:* "**Love the Lord your God with all your heart and with all your soul and with all your mind.**" *When you do this, Jesus promises to love you* *in the same manner. His love is so vast and powerful that it makes you wise, brave, strong, and intelligent!*

Imagine being asked a simple test question about your love for your parents; what would your answer be?

Which one do you love the most? *While it's true that some children feel more attached to a parent than the other, the heartfelt answer truly should be, "I love them all equally with all my heart." That's a nice way to show fairness and wisdom to both wonderful parents.*

Jesus is the best friend, because He never lies. He is the only friend who is holy. Holy means that He has no faults, He never thinks or does anything wrong, and He always protects those He loves. Psalm 18:30 says, **"As for God, His way is perfect: The Lord's word is flawless; He shields all who take refuge in Him."** You can always count on Him because He is perfect and pure. He will protect everyone who believes in him.

Since you and Jesus are now friends, your secrets are safe with Him. Jesus already knows everything about you, but He loves it when you share your thoughts and feelings with Him. Psalm 139:4 says, **"Before a word is on my tongue, you, Lord, know it completely."** You can tell Him anything, your dreams, your worries, joys, and He will keep them safe in His heart. *He will also tell you what to do.*

For example, if you want a joyful Christmas, hope to receive a special gift, need healing for yourself or someone you love, or want to get good grades at school, you can tell Jesus all these things.

Philippians 4:6 says, "*Do not be anxious about anything, but in every situation, tell me with prayer and small conversations, with thanksgiving, present your requests to God.*"

Your secrets are safe with Him, and after every prayer, you will feel a sense of happiness and peace within.

Now you might ask, "When should I pray and how should I pray to my friend Jesus?" The answer is simple: anytime and anywhere! You can pray silently in your heart, whisper little words, or talk out loud when you're alone. Matthew 6:6 says, "*But when you pray, go into your room, close the door, and pray to your unseen Father. Then your father, who sees what is done in secret, will reward you for what you are asking.*" Jesus loves to hear from you all the time.

Remember: when you pray, it's not just about saying words. You're having an honest conversation with your best friend, Jesus. You can laugh, cry, or talk to Him about your day. He listens carefully and loves you more than anyone else ever could. So, start today by speaking to Jesus, and let His love fill your heart! Let him know what is going on with you.

Chapter Ten
Children's Faith in Jesus

No Child Left Behind

HEAVENLY CITIZEN

Jesus once shared something important with His friends. In Matthew 18:3, He was talking to the growing up and said, "I tell you the truth: unless you change and become like little children, you will never enter the kingdom of heaven."

This means God wants them to come to Him with hearts like children, full of trust, kindness, honesty, and love. These are the qualities of Jesus' friends. His friends are loyal, very special, and honest. They possess a lot of wisdom; if you ask them something, they will tell you the truth, whether they know it or not.

Jesus wasn't saying we should act foolishly or childishly, but that we should always believe in Him with a pure and open heart, just like children do, because children are His most faithful friends. He hears them from the kingdom of heaven.

Jesus was speaking to grown-ups when He said this, and He wanted them to understand that having a proud or selfish heart keeps them away from God. But children are different; we believe easily, forgive quickly, and know how to love everyone. God loves it when we pray with simple words and come to Him with faith that says, "Jesus, I trust You!" Just like Gershom does in his prayers.

Jesus teaches us to love one another. In 1 John 4:7-8, he says:

"Dear friends, let us love one another, for love comes from God. Everyone who loves has been born of God and knows God. Whoever does not love does not know God, because God is love."

This means that when we are loving and kind to others, whether we are helping someone, showing respect for our parents, sharing something, forgiving a friend, or speaking good words, we are showing people what God's love looks like.

You can make a big difference. You are never too young to be a light in the world! When you love your family, help your teacher, share with your classmates, or pray for someone who is hurting, you are letting Jesus' love shine through you. God sees everything you do, and He smiles when you act with love and kindness. That is your way of making a difference in the world by caring for others.

One way to stay close to Jesus is to keep Him in your heart every day. *Whether you're doing homework, taking a big test, or helping your mom at home,* Jesus is always ready to help you. He gives us wisdom and intelligence. He helps Children remember what we studied, and He fills our minds with good thoughts so that we can learn and grow. When we walk with him, *we become strong, bright, and full of peace.*

No Child Left Behind

Have you ever heard the phrase "**No Child Left Behind**"? *It became a special law in the United States to ensure that every child, regardless of their location, has the opportunity* to learn and succeed in school.

Before the law, some schools in *poorer neighborhoods* lacked the same books, good teachers, or resources as schools in *wealthier cities*. Wealthier means *wealthy or affluent.* This meant some children were not receiving the education they deserved. However, the government decided to change that, so every child across the country could have a fair and equal education: the same books, the same school calendar and curriculum, good teachers, and an excellent education.

The **"No Child Left Behind Act"** became law when it was passed by the **United States Congress in 2002,** signed by the *43rd President of the United States,* **George W. Bush.** He said, *"We will leave no child behind.*

We will make sure every child learns to read and succeed in school." That's a wonderful goal, and it's something Jesus would love to!

The **"No Child Left Behind Act"** became law when it was passed by the **United States Congress in 2002,** signed by the *43rd President of the United States,* **George W. Bush.** He said, *"We will leave no child behind. We will make sure every child learns to read and succeed in school."* That's a wonderful goal, and it's something Jesus would love to!

Because **President Bush is a Christian**, and he is also a friend of Jesus.

When we love Jesus, He helps us learn, grow, and serve others. *He doesn't want any child left behind*, whether in school, in life, or in **His kingdom**. So, let's continue to love Him, learn more each day, and help others succeed, because with Jesus, every child matters; every child is loved and wonderfully made by God.

Dear Jesus,

Thank you for loving me and every child in the world. Help me remember that You made each of us special and important.

Please bless my teachers, friends, and classmates so we can all learn and grow together.

Show me how to help others who need a friend or a helping hand,

So that no child is ever left behind in school, in life, or in knowing You.

Thank you for making me wonderfully made.

I love You, Jesus. **Amen.**

You Are Chosen: You Are a Christian

A Christian is a person who believes in Jesus, loves Him, and wants to live like Him.

God's children grow a little every day, learning new things, meeting new friends, and trying new activities. But Jesus also wants us to succeed on the inside so that we can be strong and pure in our hearts. He says in the Bible, **"Blessed are the pure in heart, for they will see God"** (Matthew 5:8). **What would you say to him?**

That means Jesus is happy when we keep our hearts pure, **free from sinister secrets, mean thoughts, or hurtful actions.** Being pure isn't just about our bodies; it also includes the words we speak, the thoughts we have, and the choices we make. As we grow older, we should guard our hearts and minds by doing what is good, right, and proper because that's what makes Jesus smile.

Growing up means that one day, we will take on more responsibilities. We will attend high school, go to college, find a job, and even start our own businesses and families someday. But until then, we need to stay close to our parents and **trust them.**

God gave us our parents to love, guide, and protect us. Jesus said, "**Children, obey your parents in the Lord, for this is right**" (Ephesians 6:1).

This means we should always show respect to them; talk openly with Mom and Dad about things that trouble us, scare us, or make us uncomfortable. If anyone speaks badly about us or makes us feel ashamed, we should tell Mom and Dad right away. They are our haven, generously watching over us, and we believe God uses them to keep us protected.

Some things in life are private and must be protected. For example, our bodies are special and need to be treated with respect. Only a doctor is allowed to perform specific examinations or checks, and only with a parent or guardian present. "No one is allowed to see us or meet us alone," because Jesus wants us to stay in a safe environment at all times.

No one else has the right or permission to touch or look at our private parts, no matter what they say or give us. Remember, *we are children of God, and Jesus is watching over us to see how wise and kind we are. He trusts us to be smart and make good choices.* If someone ever tries to do something like that, *it's important to say no and tell our parents immediately.*

Our bodies are special because Jesus, our best friend, says, "*Your body is the house of the Holy Spirit*" (1 Corinthians 6:19).

This means that God lives in us, and it's our joy and duty to care for ourselves in ways that bring Him happiness.

There are specific conversations that Christian children should not have with anyone, particularly those involving sensitive topics. If someone tries to talk to us about things that seem strange, confusing, or that we don't understand, particularly those concerning adult life, *we should immediately tell our parents. There are some things that only Mom or Dad can explain, and they will do so with love, sincerity, and kindness.* "*When God's Word is explained, it brings light. It helps even simple hearts understand what is right.*"(Psalm 119:130).

When we share our questions and concerns with our parents, we allow God's light to help us understand what is right. Mom and Dad will always be there to explain things to you, for your good.

Guess what?

*Our parents will love us for all their days on earth. Their love can't be measured; it's bigger than we can imagine and goes on forever. **For this reason, go now and tell them how much you love them.***

Staying in school also shows good behavior. God wants us to be wise and prepared for the future. Jesus teaches Christian children to be smart academically: He said, "**Let the wise child listen and increase their knowledge, and let those who understand gain guidance**" (Proverbs 1:5).

Attending school, studying diligently, and completing our education help us prepare for future work. One day, *you'll be called Mr., Ms., Mrs., or Madam*, because you've obeyed your parents and studied hard. This will make it easier to support yourself and care for the family you'll have someday. God has excellent plans for our future, but we must be patient and focus on growing into healthy and intelligent individuals.

Until we become adults, we must continue sharing everything with our parents: our questions, feelings, mistakes, and joys. They are our first teachers at home, guiding us through every stage of life. Moses said, "**Our parents will train the children in the way they should go, and when they grow up, they will not depart from it**" (Proverbs 22:6). This shows that our parents help shape our future, and it is vital to listen and learn from them while we are young.

Jesus wants every child to stay safe at all times. Whether we are at school, on the playground, at a friend's house, or online, we need to use wisdom and make decisions that protect us. If something seems unusual, scary, or dangerous, we should report it. "*I will say to the Lord, 'You are my safe place and my helper. You are my God, and I trust you.'*" (Psalm 91:2). We can only trust Jesus. He uses our parents as trusted adults, such as teachers and doctors, to protect us, but *we also need to be brave enough to tell them*

truth and ask for help when necessary.

Being pure also means being careful about what we listen to and watch on television or online. Some songs, videos, or games are not suitable for the growth of our hearts as Christians.

Gabe, **Isaiah**, and their little brother **Gershom** are proud Christians. They've learned to read the Bible and often ask their parents many questions, demonstrating their curiosity and faith. They remember the verse, "*I will set no foolish thing before my eyes*" (Psalm 101:3), which reminds us that it's important not to watch things that are harmful or unkind.

It's perfectly okay to say no to anything that doesn't help us grow closer to Jesus. When in doubt, we can ask our parents for guidance to make safe and healthy choices. Keeping ourselves pure also means choosing good friends who want to do what's right, helping us stay on the right path and live with kindness.

God wants us to grow strong in faith, kind in heart, and wise in mind. Being pure doesn't mean we're perfect, but it means we choose to follow God's way, even when it's hard. We may sometimes make mistakes, but we can always turn to God and our parents for help, guidance, and forgiveness.

"If we confess our sins, he is faithful and just to forgive us our sins and to cleanse us from all unrighteousness" (1 John 1:9). Staying pure inside is something we do every day by walking closely with Jesus.

As we grow up, remember this: *our hearts, minds, and bodies are gifts from God.* We protect them by staying close to Jesus, sharing everything with our parents, and making wise choices. We wait patiently for the day when we are old enough to take on adult responsibilities.

But until then, we walk in purity, truth, and love. *"Don't let anyone look down on you because you are young, but set an example for the believers in speech, in conduct, in love, in faith, and purity"* (1 Timothy 4:12). *You are a child of God, and He is proud of you!*

Chapter Eleven

Why Jesus Loves Children, we are friends

We show his Love to others.

HEAVENLY CITIZEN

The love of family and friends.

John was one of Jesus' younger brothers; they shared the same parents. He was also among the twelve closest friends and disciples of Jesus. John consistently upheld what is right; he overheard some individuals speaking lies about his brother, and he responded in John 4:8: « **If you don't have love, you don't know my brother Jesus, because Jesus is love!** »

God created families and friendships to be filled with love, laughter, and care for one another. The Lord Jesus says, "**Love each other like brothers and sisters. Be the best at showing kindness and respect to one another.**" (Romans 12:10).

Whenever I spend time with my cousins **Nicia, Ketia, Nilsa, and Olivia**, we talk about our love for Jesus, and it feels like we're wrapped in God's big hug. Loving Jesus makes us even closer as a family. He's not only our Savior, but also our best friend, and He fills our hearts with peace and joy.

My cousins are some of the kindest and most amazing kids you could ever meet! We always have so much fun playing together, and *I'm so thankful God gave me such a beautiful and wonderful family.* How about you? Can you tell me about your brothers and sisters?

As Christian children, we are called to love with a pure heart. 1 Timothy 1:5 says, "**The most important thing the Lord Jesus teaches is love. Why?** This love comes from a pure heart, a clear mind, and a true faith."

When I am with my best friends, Accisah, Josh, and Abiellah, we feel love and are very happy. They are older than my brother and me, but they always treat me with kindness and respect. Their passion is friendly; they are

Christians as well. That's what makes it special and real.

The Angels' Voices on My Birthday

My name is Gershom, and my older brother is Isaiah. We love celebrating birthdays with family and friends. Gabe, our older brother and the firstborn, also enjoys traveling on special days, so birthdays often turn into mini family adventures. In our family, birthdays aren't just about balloons, cakes, gifts, or parties; they're about gathering together, thanking God for our lives, calling each other to express love, and sharing joy with those we cherish most.

For us, birthdays are the most cherished family moments. We love traveling from house to house to see the person, exchanging small gifts, and sharing kind words that bring a smile to everyone's face. Yet, the most meaningful gift isn't something you can buy; it's when we all hug each other, pray together, and cheerfully say, "*Happy Birthday!*" That moment feels like love wrapping us in warmth. My father always leads us in prayer, thanking God for life and asking for His blessings on the birthday person.

Psalm 90:12:

"So, teach us to number our days, that we may apply our hearts unto wisdom."

My Funny Dad

Now, let me tell you about my dad. He's the funniest person in the world, or at least, that's what he thinks, ha ha! Every year since we were little, he has had his own way of making birthdays unforgettable. When I turned seven, he bought a giant hat that looked like a birthday cake with candles on top and made me wear it the whole day. When Isaiah turned nine, Dad surprised him by singing "**Happy Birthday**" in three different languages, even though he only really knew a few words in each one!

But the best part? He insists that no birthday is complete without his "special birthday story." Each year, he tells us a story about how God made us unique and how our lives are like chapters in a book that He is still writing. Even though the story changes slightly each year, the message remains the same: God gave us life for a purpose, and each birthday serves as a reminder of His love.

Psalm 118:24:

"**This is the day which the Lord hath made; we will rejoice**

and be glad in it."

Birthdays in our house are full of small traditions. Dad decorates the living room the night before, and Mom prepares a surprise dish. It might be cake or our favorite food, it's always a bit of a mystery. He calls it "**a special gift for my beautiful Queen,**" because he feels that celebrating us also honors her love and effort as a mother.

Our family has a tradition of choosing a different location for each birthday celebration, whether it's a park, a beach, or our backyard transformed into a "birthday camp" with tents and fairy lights. No matter where we are, it feels magical because we're together. Dad often says, "It's not the place that makes the day special; it's the people who fill it with joy."

Gabe usually leads us in fun games, Isaiah cracks jokes, and I'm usually the one who eats too much cake and gets caught! But no matter what, birthdays in our home always end with laughter, music, and prayer.

Lessons from Birthdays

What I love most about birthdays isn't the presents, but the love we share. Our father always reminds us: "***The best gift is not what you hold in your hands, but what you hold in your heart.***" That means how we treat each other is more important than any toy or gadget. A kind word like "***I love you,***" "***thank you,***" or "***I'm proud of you***" is more valuable than any gift. These words are like hugs for the heart, and they show that we belong to each other.

Most importantly, I forgot to tell you that my grandma Anna is both a hugger and a poet of love. She possesses one of the greatest gifts God can give, the ability to lift others with encouragement. As an elder, she always aimed to present herself with grace, even wearing a fragrance so pleasant that no one in the family would ever miss the chance to embrace her. We love her dearly, and every moment spent with her feels like another blessing poured out from the Lord.

Jesus Himself taught us this. In John 13:34, He said:

"A new commandment I give unto you, that ye love one another; as I have loved you, that ye also love one another. Birthdays remind us that love is the greatest gift of all. They are not just about getting older; they are about growing deeper in love, kindness, and understanding.

Why Jesus Loves Children

Do you know why Jesus loves children so much?

Because children have hearts that are open, trusting, and pure, when the disciples once tried to keep children away, Jesus said:

"Suffer the little children to come unto me, and forbid them not: for of such is the kingdom of God" (Mark 10:14). Jesus loves birthdays, too, because they celebrate life, and life itself is His gift to us.

John 6:35:

"And Jesus said unto them, I am the bread of life: he that cometh to me shall never hunger; and he that believeth on me shall never thirst."

Every time we gather for a birthday, I picture Jesus smiling down, happy to see families united in love. He understands that when we celebrate one another, we are also celebrating Him, because He is the source of all life.

On birthdays, my dad always makes sure we remember others, not just ourselves. He reminds us to share happiness with others. Sometimes that means giving a slice of cake to a neighbor, calling a relative, or visiting someone who might be lonely. He says, **"If God gave us another year of life, we should use it to bless others."**

Proverbs 11:25 says:

"The liberal soul shall be made fat: and he that watereth shall be watered also himself."

In other words, when you bless others, you are blessed in return. Birthdays are the perfect opportunity to do that. One year, instead of giving gifts, our family collected clothes and toys to donate to children in need. It was the best birthday ever because giving made us feel happier than receiving.

So, whether it's a birthday, a family trip, or just a simple dinner at home, what matters most is the love we share. True happiness in a family doesn't come from money, big houses, or fancy cars. It comes from the small, everyday moments, laughing together, praying and forgiving each other, and supporting each other through every season of life.

Each birthday reminds us that we are **citizens of God's Kingdom**. Our life isn't just about the years we count on earth, but about the love we share and the legacy we leave behind. As Psalm 90:12, King David says: *"So teach us to number our days, that we may apply our hearts unto wisdom."*

So, my friend, when your birthday comes, remember this: your life is a gift from God, and your love is a gift to others, with no wrapping paper, no bow, just kindness, joy, and a heart full of faith.

Chapter Twelve

The love of grandparents

Why Is Respect
So Important?

HEAVENLY CITIZEN

The love of grandparents

Our parents are also part of this wonderful circle. The Bible says, "*Grandchildren are a special joy to grandparents, and children feel proud because of their parents.*" (Proverbs 17:6). The fact that our parents are Christian and Jesus' best friends means that we grow up in an atmosphere of peace and harmony. Jesus uses our families to protect us, guide us, and remind us that we are never alone.

Having parents who love Jesus is one of life's most secure and robust gifts. Jesus taught children to love one another as we love ourselves. In 1 John 4:8, he says, "*God is love. If we love others, it shows we know God.*" So, you must love one another. I think of my grandparents, Grandma *Concessa* and Grandpa *Faustin*, and the unconditional, profound love they gave us.

They are God's blessing and the guardians of my life. Their love teaches me what it means to care for someone without asking for anything in return, just as Jesus does. *All of my love goes to them; may they be blessed forever.*

Do you love your grandparents too?

Please share with us!

Uncles and aunts are also part of this big family blessing. Ils sont : **Mozy, Cédric, Feza, Denise, Longin, Donald, Marjorie, Herline, Frédérick, Cherline et Nadia. Carline, Myriam, Enude.**

I am truly grateful. They are like extra parents. They guide us, pray for us, play with us, and show us new things.

Proverbs 27:9 says:

"Good friends bring joy to your heart, just like sweet smells make you happy. Accurate advice comes from love and their sincere counsel.

Family is all about giving heartfelt advice filled with love, helping each of us grow and thrive. That's the essence of what a Christian family stands for.

Then there's my big brother Gabe. We call him 'Mr. Gabe, because he's so much like Dad, kind, charming, and respectful. He's already learned to be warm and polite. He already acts like my second dad! He's funny, loving, and strong.

Sometimes he forgets he's not in charge, but I love him anyway, because he's just trying to protect me; he's my big brother. His favorite words are

"Gershom, come here now, you hear?". That's what Jesus does, too!

In Ephesians 4:32, He said:

"Be kind and compassionate to one another, forgiving each other, just as in Christ God forgave you."

My brother's heart is full of love, and that makes me feel safe and happy to be around him.

The love we share within our family and among our Christian friends isn't ordinary; that is God's love shining through us. When we gather to pray, play, or laugh, that love David was singing about. Psalm 133:1: **"How good and pleasant it is when brothers live together in unity!"** This unity acts like a warm blanket that shields us in Jesus, brings us joy, and draws us nearer to God.

Being born into a Christian family is a blessing. Our faith isn't just something we talk about; it guides how we live, love, and forgive. Colossians 3:14 says, **"And above all these virtues, clothe yourselves with love, which binds**

them all together in perfect unity." That's what makes my family so special: we are all connected through Jesus, and nothing can break that bond.

If I could grant one wish for every child, it would be this: to grow up in a family like mine, *where everyone is friends with Jesus, love is real, and we all help each other walk with God.* I know that not everyone is so fortunate, which is why I am always grateful to God.

Psalm 100:5 says:

"*For the Lord is good and his love endures forever; his faithfulness continues through all generations.*" Jesus placed me in this family for a reason, and that reason is love. I aim to tell my story and remind every child that they are loved and wonderfully made, just as they are, by our Lord Jesus Christ.

Now it's your turn to share! We'd like to know more about your family: who do you love spending *time with?*

Do you have a favorite holiday where you laugh, eat good food, and give thanks to God? Gershom, Isaiah, Gabe, and Jesus are listening to you with open hearts. Everything you say is safe with us: your secrets are precious, and we will keep them among friends. The Bible says, "**A true friend loves you all the time, and a brother is there when things get tough.**"(Proverbs 17:17). That means, no matter what happens, we are here to love and support you!

We send you all our love, to you and your family, from our hearts to yours, and the love of our Lord Jesus Christ. We hope your home is filled with joy and peace. We pray that you do your best at school to earn good grades, and that Jesus will give you wisdom and strength to be intelligent and make good choices every day.

Jesus said: For the Lord gives wisdom to every child, from his mouth comes knowledge and understanding.

He made all Christian children intelligent for a reason, so that they can help others. Never forget that you are thoughtful, kind, and exceptional in God's eyes. May He heal you, if you are hurt or sad, whether in your heart or your body.

Dear Jesus,
Thank you for loving me so much.
Please heal my body and keep me healthy.
Give me a brilliant mind and a heart full of wisdom,
So, I can help other children learn, grow, and be happy.
Help me share Your love with my friends every day.
In your name, I pray. **Amen.**

If you don't know Jesus yet, or if your family doesn't talk about Him, *that's okay*; you can still choose Him for yourself! Jesus loves you so much, and He is waiting to be your best friend.

The Lord Jesus says, "*If you believe in your heart and confess with your mouth that Jesus is Lord, you will be saved*" (Romans 10:9). You can tell Him in your own words, "*Jesus, I want You to be my friend and my Savior. I believe in You!*" That is how you will become a member of His eternal family in God's Kingdom.

Then, you will be a **Christian, you'll be one of 2.9 billion followers of Jesus.** From now on, **you can walk confidently as a Christian, a child of the Most-High God, and a citizen of heaven.** You don't have to be shy or afraid to say, "*I love you, Jesus!*" He is always with you, wherever you go. Jesus says, "*I am with you always*" (Matthew 28:20). You are never alone. You now have a large family of faith that includes **Gabe, Gershom, and Isaiah**, all of God's children. **Welcome to the team!** Jesus is smiling because you are his new friend, a Christian, and a citizen of heaven!

The Wisdom of Elders: God's Gift to Children

When you hear the word "wisdom," **what comes to mind?**

Maybe you think of school, books, intelligence, or a teacher explaining a lesson. But did you know that one of the most important sources of wisdom God has given us is right inside our homes and families?

Yes, it comes through the voices of our grandparents, parents, guardians, step-parents, uncles, aunts, and even our older brothers and sisters. These are the people God places in our lives to guide us, protect us, and teach us lessons that last forever. They are direct guidance from his heavenly kingdom. The Bible states in Proverbs 1:8:

"My son, hear the instruction of thy father, and forsake not the law of thy mother." God wants us to listen carefully to the older people in our lives because they possess knowledge and experience that we have not yet gained. Respecting them isn't just good manners; it is part of being a good child of God.

Why Is Respect So Important?

It is more than just saying "**please**" and "**thank you**." Respect is demonstrated when you listen, obey, and treat others with kindness. A good child of God shows respect not only to teachers at school or coaches on a team, but especially to the elders in their family. **Why?** Because elders have traveled the road of life much longer than we have. *They know what joy feels like, what mistakes cost, and what wisdom is necessary to grow.*

When you respect your elders, you are truly honoring God.

Exodus 20:12 states:

"Honor thy father and thy mother: that thy days may be long upon the land which the Lord thy God giveth thee." *Respecting others brings blessings. It shows God that you are humble and willing to learn, and He rewards that spirit with a good life.*

Why Elders' Words Last a Lifetime

Have you ever noticed how people often quote their grandparents or parents long after they're gone?

Someone might say, "My grandmother *always said...*" or "My *dad used to remind me...*" Those words persist because they carried truth, love, and wisdom. Wise words don't fade away; they become seeds planted in our hearts.

Wisdom means using what you know to make good choices that please God and help others. It's like having a guide in your heart that shows you the right thing to do, even when it's hard.

Researchers at universities have even studied this. They found that children who grew up listening to their grandparents' or parents' stories remembered them for many years. Even after those elders passed away, the children carried their lessons into adulthood. That means wisdom is like a *treasure chest, a secret and a gift to every child*: once it's given to you, *it belongs to you forever.*

So, next time your grandmother tells you a story or your dad repeats a lesson for the tenth time, don't roll your eyes. Pay attention! Those words might be the very ones you'll carry with you for the rest of your life.

Why Grandparents Feel Like Home

Have you ever felt that exceptional warmth when visiting your grandparents? There's something about **their**

hugs, cooking, or even just the way they **smile** at you that makes you feel safe and loved. Children often feel at home around their grandparents because they embody patience, gentleness, and unconditional love. They usually don't rush; they listen. They've lived long enough to understand that love matters more than being busy.

The Bible tells us in Proverbs 17:6:

"Children's children are the crown of old men, and parents are the pride of their children." This means grandparents see their grandchildren as their reward and joy. They love to give, nurture, and watch their family grow. That's why you can always go back to their home, and they will welcome you with open arms. Their love reflects God's love, always open, always willing to forgive, always ready to embrace.

Do you see how Jesus' love shines through our elders?

Grandparents, parents, uncles, aunties, and even older brothers and sisters often carry His love in their hearts, just for us to discover. Every hug, story, and piece of advice is like a treasure chest filled with God's love, **waiting for us to explore.** When we listen to and respect them, we aren't just learning about life; we are also learning how much Jesus loves us through the people He placed in our family.

It's not just grandparents who carry this wisdom. *Step-parents, guardians, uncles, and aunties* also play a significant role in shaping children's lives. Sometimes God uses them as extra voices of care and guidance when parents are not around. **Older siblings**, too, can guide us, even if they don't always get it right. They've walked ahead of us in school, friendships, and life choices. By watching them, we can learn what to do, and sometimes what not to do!

Each of these elders is like *a lamp that God has placed in our path*. Their light helps us walk straight and avoid stumbling. When we ignore them, it's like walking in the **dark without a flashlight**. But when we listen to and respect them, our steps are guided by both their wisdom and God's truth.

What It Means to Be a Good Child of God

Being a faithful child or a good child of God involves more than just reading the Bible and praying; it also means showing respect in everyday life. When your grandma needs help with groceries, you don't wait to be asked; you take initiative. If your parents tell you to finish your homework before playing, you do so cheerfully. When your aunt shares a story from her childhood, you listen patiently without *interrupting*.

These small actions show that you value the **wisdom** God has given your family.

Jesus Himself showed respect to His earthly parents.

In **Luke 2:51**, the Bible says:

"And he went down with them, and came to Nazareth, and was subject unto them." Even though Jesus was the Son of God, He still obeyed Mary and Joseph. If Jesus could respect His parents, how much more should we?

One day, your grandparents or parents may no longer be with you, but their words will stay. You will remember their advice, encouragement, and love. Those memories will give you strength when life feels tough. They will remind you of who you are and whose you are, a child of God.

So, listen carefully now. Respect deeply. Treasure their stories and their love. Because one day, you might be the elder in someone else's life. You might be the one whose words get quoted years later. You might be the one who hugs a grandchild and makes them feel at home.

Wisdom from elders is one of the greatest gifts God gives us. Parents, guardians, grandparents, uncles, aunties, and older siblings all carry lessons that can help us live better, love more deeply, and follow God more closely. Respecting them is not just about being polite; it is about being a good child of God, honoring Him by treating others with respect.

So, the next time your grandparent hugs you, your parent gives advice, or your older sibling teaches you something, take a moment to thank God. Because every word of wisdom, every hug, and every lesson is another blessing from the Lord.

Dear Heavenly Father,

Thank you for the wisdom of our elders, our grandparents, parents, guardians, step-parents, uncles, aunties, and older brothers and sisters. You have placed them in our lives as gifts from Your Kingdom to guide us, protect us, and teach us lessons that will last forever.

Lord, help me to respect them in every way, not just by saying "please" and "thank you," but by listening, obeying, and showing kindness. Remind me that when I honor my elders, I am also honoring You, just as You commanded in Your Word: *"Honour thy father and thy mother, that thy days may be long"* (Exodus 20:12).

Thank you to our grandparents whose hugs feel like home, whose smiles remind us of Your love, and whose stories stay in our hearts even after they are gone. Thank you to our parents and guardians who guide us, to our older siblings who walk before us, and to every elder who shines like a lamp on our path.

Lord Jesus, just as You obeyed Mary and Joseph, help me to walk in obedience, humility, and love. Teach me to value the words of my elders, knowing that one day I may be the one whose words guide others.

I thank You for every lesson, story, and act of love. Each one is a blessing from You. Please continue to bless my family, friends, and everyone who helps me grow as a child of God.

In Jesus' name I pray, **Amen.**

Now, it's your turn to send your prayer request to Jesus. Dear Jesus,

----

Amen

Chapter Thirteen

My Home Is a Healing Place

What does it mean to be a Christian child? We belong to the Kingdom.

HEAVENLY CITIZEN

My Home Is a Healing Place

God's love fills our entire home like sunlight, bringing us warmth, peace, and joy. It reminds us every day that He is with us, caring for us, and making our home a little piece of heaven. Our home feels like a cozy nest, soft, safe, and full of peace. Joy comes from every little thing: *warm hugs, bedtime prayers, shared meals, and lots of laughter.* When I feel weak or sad, I know I can find rest in this special place God has given me, because I am very grateful to have a Christian family and friends.

King David says, "*He will cover you with His feathers, and under His wings, you will find refuge*" (Psalm 91:4). Mommy says that our home isn't perfect, but it is filled with **God's love**, and that makes it enough to help us grow strong in spirit.

When something troubles me, I don't need to hide it. My parents always say that we shouldn't keep secrets from each other, especially not from Jesus. Jesus told His friend in Luke 8:17, "*For there is nothing hidden that will not be disclosed, and nothing concealed that will not be known or brought out into the open.*"

Did you know that Jesus knows everything, even the things hiding in our minds? I used to think I was too big to cry or too strong to talk about my feelings, but Mommy and Daddy tell me that being honest and open is how real strength grows. Even Jesus cried in John 11:35, saying, Jesus wept", and He was never ashamed to talk to His Father.

Sometimes, I feel funny when I act like a little child around Mommy and Daddy, even though I'm getting older. But Daddy told me that's okay, I can always go to him. In Matthew 18:3, Jesus said, "*Truly I tell you, unless you change and become like little children, you will never enter the kingdom of heaven.*" Being childlike in love and trust is not a weakness; it's the strength that comes from knowing you're fully loved.

So even though the world outside can be confusing or even scary, my home is my strong tower. Just like King Solomon said in Proverbs 18:10, "The name of the Lord is a strong tower; the righteous run to it and are safe." My family talks, prays, and looks out for each other. *Daddy says we have to stay alert because being alert helps keep us safe and wise.* But even more than that, we trust Jesus to guard our hearts and guide our steps. And every night, before we sleep, we know that love, God's love, is still holding us close.

The Power of Loving Touch and Healing Words from my Parents

Hello, friends. Are *you a friend of Jesus*? When you're in trouble, *do you have someone you can fully trust to talk to?* For me, that person is my parents. Mommy's hugs feel like warm sunshine on a cloudy day. Her arms wrap around me, and all the bad feelings melt away. Daddy's words are like a strong arm; they lift me when I feel down and help me smile again. My dad has a great gift, and I love being around him. He has a charismatic voice that encourages me whenever I'm feeling down or having a bad day.

Their gentle hands wipe my tears, and their kind voices remind me that I am safe and loved. Just like Jesus says, "**Pleasant words are a honeycomb, sweet to the soul and healing to the bones**" (Proverbs 16:24). When

Mommy and Daddy speak kindly, it's like Jesus is talking through them. I pray that you have a good relationship with your parents or guardians as well.

Jesus' love is profoundly influential. It can heal every heart when individuals feel sorrowful or unwell. It dispels fears and restores courage. In times of difficulty or despair, *it is essential to pray to God for healing.* Jesus always knows the appropriate words and actions to assist. I believe that God bestowed upon parents a special gift for healing, just as Jesus healed people in the Bible, through love and kindness.

Daddy always reminds us to take good care of our bodies. He says, *"Our bodies are the temple of God,"* **and that means we should be careful with what we eat, drink, and think about.** God made us special, and we should treat ourselves with the respect we deserve. Our little brother Gershom asks Daddy many questions, and sometimes his questions make all of us laugh. But Daddy always gives the best answers.

One day, he asked, "How do we know that God is holy?" Daddy smiled and said, "Do you eat fruit?" Gershom replied, "Yes, what's that have to do with holiness?" Daddy asked, "Is there any fruit that doesn't have a cover?" Gershom thought hard and said, "**No.**" Daddy explained, "God wraps all the food He gives us with a covering like peels or shells to keep it safe from the rain, the bugs, and the dirt.

God's holiness means that God's heart is always clean and good. He loves what is right and never does wrong, and He teaches us to protect what is good, just as He does. That's how we know He is full of love and goodness." Gershom's eyes opened wide, and he said, "God is an awesome God!"

Mommy was so moved by what my brother said that she asked him to say a prayer.

She said, "Let's thank God for all the ways He protects us, just like the skin on a fruit." We all nodded, closed our eyes, folded our hands, and began to pray. It was a brief prayer, but it filled everyone with warmth. We all felt the love of Jesus in that moment, in our living room, surrounded by hugs and laughter.

What does it mean to be a Christian child?

Being a Christian child can sometimes be challenging, but at other times it feels like the most incredible adventure. Each day offers new trials and blessings, and with Jesus by our side, every step becomes a journey of faith, bravery, and happiness. A safe place to return to daily is like a little piece of heaven on earth. For children, a loving home filled with kindness, peace, and prayer is one of God's greatest blessings.

Not all children worldwide have this gift, which is why Christian children are encouraged to be grateful, pray for others, and live with open hearts. The Bible reminds us:

"Every good and perfect gift is from above, coming down from the Father of the heavenly lights" (James 1:17). Our homes, families, and friendships are part of these blessings. Recognizing them as gifts from God helps us treat them with care, respect, and thankfulness.

I am being alert and wise.

Being a Christian child means we need to be thoughtful and attentive, not only in school but also in our daily lives. God has placed us in a world where not everything is safe, and not everyone can be trusted. That's why it's so important to stay alert, recognize what is good and what is wrong, and learn which people we can trust.

Proverbs 4:23 teaches:

"Above all else, guard your heart, for everything you do flows from it."

This means we need to watch our thoughts, feelings, and choices, because they shape who we are. A wise child learns not to follow bad influences but to seek what is pure and good.

Being intelligent isn't just about knowing facts; it's about possessing the wisdom of God. Wisdom surpasses gold or silver in value. "For the Lord gives wisdom; from his mouth come knowledge and understanding" (Proverbs 2:6). When we listen to God, we gain insight that far exceeds anything we could learn on our own.

Friendship with Jesus is the most intelligent decision for every child.

Being a friend of Jesus is more than just becoming a Christian or claiming to believe. Friendship with Jesus entails walking with Him each day, sharing your heart in prayer, and learning His words to guide you in living.

Jesus Himself said:

"You are my friends if you do what I command" (John 15:14). He does not call us servants, but friends. As children of God, we belong to His heavenly kingdom, and we are part of His family forever.

Being His friend makes us strong and confident. It brings us peace when we are afraid, joy when we are sad, and courage when we are unsure. A true friend never leaves, and Jesus promises: "Surely I am with you always, to the very end of the age" (Matthew 28:20).

As children of God, we also become more alert and aware of our surroundings. We start to recognize the difference between right and wrong. We learn to choose honesty over lying, kindness over anger, and faith over fear.

Paul wrote to young Timothy:

"Don't let anyone look down on you because you are young, but set an example for the believers in speech, in conduct, in love, in faith, and in purity" (1 Timothy 4:12). This verse shows that even children can be leaders in

God's Kingdom by demonstrating what it means to live for Christ.

Knowing God makes us truly smart in a way the world can't measure. Smartness isn't just about getting good grades; it's about understanding God's Word and living by it. "The fear of the Lord is the beginning of wisdom, and knowledge of the Holy One is understanding" (Proverbs 9:10).

Protecting ourselves and every other child under Jesus's
supervision.

God wants His children to stay safe. This means we need to learn how to protect ourselves from harm. Sometimes that involves speaking up when something is wrong, telling a trusted adult, or avoiding danger. God gives us wisdom so we can make good decisions.

King Solomon said in Proverbs 27:12:

"**Smart kids see trouble coming and stay safe, but foolish kids keep going and get hurt.**" If we notice something unsafe, we should act wisely, whether that means telling a teacher, parent, asking for help, the police, or walking away.

But our responsibility doesn't end with ourselves. God calls us to pray for and protect others as well. Jesus teaches us to love our neighbors as ourselves (Mark

12:31). That includes every child in the world who longs for a safe home, a caring family, and the joy of friendship.

Praying for All Children

As Christian children, our prayers are powerful. James 5:16 tells us:

"The prayer of a righteous child is powerful and effective." When we pray for other children, God listens. We can ask Him to give every boy and girl a good home, loving parents, and safety when they travel or go to school.

Jesus cares profoundly for children. He said, "Let the little children come to me, and do not hinder them, for the kingdom of heaven belongs to such as these" (Matthew 19:14). Every child is important to Him, and when we pray, we demonstrate our love and support for them, aligning with Jesus' caring heart.

We should pray for children who are poor, sick, or lonely, asking God to send them hope and healing. We should pray for children living in dangerous places that God will keep them safe. And we should pray for children who do not yet know Jesus, that they will discover His love and become part of His family.

Life with God involves not just facing challenges, but also experiencing joy and adventure. Family moments, whether after school, during a fun game, or while traveling, become opportunities to celebrate God's goodness.

Psalm 133:1 says:

"How wonderful and joyful it is when God's people live in unity!" As families laugh, pray, and share experiences, they forge memories that mirror the happiness of heaven. Even simple activities, such as family meals or walks in the park, can become sacred moments when we recall God's presence with us.

With the Lord, everything is possible. "*With God all things are possible*" (Matthew 19:26). Even the most significant challenges can turn into victories when we trust Him. Even the hardest days can end with hope when we lean on His promises.

We are the Kingdom Children.

Being a Christian child means living with courage, wisdom, and joy. It cannot be easy at times, but it is also the most fantastic adventure of all. With Jesus as our friend, we are never alone. With God's Word as our guide, we are always ready. With the Holy Spirit in our hearts, we are forever loved.

So, remember, dear child: You are a son or daughter of the King of Kings. You are part of His Kingdom now and forever. Live wisely, stay alert, protect yourself, pray for others, and enjoy every adventure with your family and with the Lord.

For it is written: *"I can do all things through Christ who strengthens me"* (Philippians 4:13).

Gershom Prayed,
Heavenly Father,
Jesus, thank you for my family.
My dad and mom are fantastic; please bless them.
My brothers are amazing. Please bless them, too.
And bless every child in the world. Give them peace, hugs, and protection.
Please give them a lot of food to eat.
In your name I pray, Jesus. Amen

Chapter Fourteen

What Would Jesus Do?

Morality of right and wrong

HEAVENLY CITIZEN

Que ferait Jésus?

"If you have what you need and you see someone who needs help, but you don't help them, is God's love really in your heart?

Dear friends, **don't just say you love people, show it by how you act and how you treat them.**"

We may be children, *but we are capable of telling right from wrong.* God did not create us too young to care about others; Jesus gave us big hearts, even in our small bodies! When we see someone in need, even if we don't have what they need ourselves, we can still do something. We can care about them. *We can discuss this with our parents.*

We can pray. Being a child doesn't mean we are powerless. Jesus loves it when children help others, because it shows how much we understand his love.

One day at school, my brother Gershom and I noticed something unusual. *A boy arrived wearing dirty clothes. His shoes were worn out, and his backpack appeared old and worn.* The other children started laughing and pointing at him. This made us feel sad. Without hesitation, Gershom and I looked at each other at the same time and said, "What would Jesus do?" This question guided us on what to do next.

We're not just ordinary children; we're friends of Jesus, and we knew in our hearts he would help the boy. We went to the boy and stood by him, telling the others, **"He is our friend."** The boy was surprised and shy, but when he smiled, he showed us that we made the right choice— sometimes, doing what's proper means supporting someone when no one else will.

Later that day, when we got home, we told our dad what had happened. If you remember, our dad is a very generous man of God. He always says, *"Giving is the fastest way to receive more from God.*" He listened to our story carefully, and the first thing he said was, "*What do you need to help your friend?*" I blinked. Did he say that? *Yes*, he did. He wanted to help us!

Gershom said, "*Isaiah, we're going to help this boy.*" It felt good to do something kind. His name was Little James.

Guess what? Gabe wanted to help, too! He was in middle school, but he came over to join us. When he asked the boy's name, we told him, "**His name is Little James.**"

Gabe smiled and said, "*That's not his real name.*"

He walked up to the boy and said, "*Hi, what's your name?*"

The boy replied, "*My name is Little James.*"

Gabe shook his head and said, "*That's not your name, boy. From now on, your name is Mr. James.*"

The boy grinned from ear to ear and kept saying, "**My name is Mr. James!**"

You know what? It's just like when you become a Christian, Jesus gives you a new name. **You become a citizen of His heavenly Kingdom,** and you suddenly have about 2.9 billion brothers and sisters around the world who love you!

We went shopping! Not for ourselves, but for our new friend. We bought him a new *backpack, new shoes, clean clothes, and school supplies.* And the best part? The next day, our friend came to school all smiles, well-dressed, and sat with us in the cafeteria. *He no longer sat alone.* He now had friends, the friends of Jesus.

Now, *let me ask you this*: What would you do if you were in our place? Would you keep walking or help? *Have you ever helped a friend in need?* Helping can be as simple as sharing your pencil or as significant as giving someone your lunch who is hungry. The size doesn't matter; it's your heart that counts.

Jesus said that those who are blessed and have more than others should not be proud or selfish. Instead, *they should stay humble and seek ways to help those who are less fortunate.* The next time you see someone in need, ask yourself, "*What would Jesus do?*" Then don't hesitate, take action. Please get involved and share with them.

If you don't have anything to give to someone in need, that's okay. You can still help by praying for them in your heart, asking God to send someone who can meet their needs. Remember, *prayer is a precious gift because it comes from a loving heart*, and God hears every single word.

Gershom said, "*Love is not just something we feel, it's something we do.*"

Let's think about this: when we share our food or give something to someone in need, it might feel like we're losing something, *but are we?* Not at all! Remember, Jesus promises to bless us in return. My dad used to say, **'Giving is the fastest way of getting back from God,' and that's so true!** Whenever the Lord blesses you, it will be a double blessing. He doesn't just return what we gave; He blesses us with double, meaning we get more than we originally shared!

Jesus once said, **"I bless you so that you can bless others."** My mom always says the same thing. I asked her one day, "Mom, why do you give your clothes and shoes to other people?" She smiled and replied, "Because I don't need them right now, and Jesus will give me better ones later." **Wow.** That's a smart way to give. *Do you give like that?* Could you please share an example of something valuable you have provided?

Now it's your turn to share. Have you ever helped someone in your family? Maybe you and your parents have given food, clothes, or a gift to someone. How did that make you feel? Let me guess: **it made you feel good.** That feeling is Jesus smiling in your heart.,

Our parents donate every year. We also **visit children's hospitals**, places where sick children receive care. Not only do our parents give to the hospital, but they also help families in need. Last time, we visited a children's hospital in Boston, Massachusetts. **Do you want to hear a funny secret?**

Here's the story: My brother Gershom struggles to say the word **"Massachusetts."** He would say "*massachouzeet*," making us all laugh, and even he enjoyed the laughter! Our dad helped him by breaking it into parts: "*Massa-chu-setts*." That sounded much better, right? But at this point, *my brother doesn't mind how he says it*, because he'll mess it up every time with a good sense of humor. Do you have any words that are hard for you to pronounce? Don't worry, Jesus understands you anyway. Please share with us...

Boston Children's Hospital is one of the best hospitals for children, not just in the United States, but in the world. It's connected to Harvard Medical School, a renowned institution where doctors learn to care for children. This hospital is special because it's a place where children receive excellent care, and doctors continually learn how to help children get better. *"Every good and perfect gift is from above" (James 1:17)*. A hospital that cares for children is a wonderful gift from God, as Jesus said, "**the kingdom of heaven belongs to children.**"

As you walk inside, it feels a lot like entering a five-star hotel. Everything shines and is spotless. The rooms are private, so each child has their own safe space. They're not just plain rooms; each one has toys, games, and books to make children feel happy while they recover. "**The joy of the Lord is every child's strength**" (Nehemiah 8:10), and sometimes that joy comes through simple things, like a good Christian book like this one or a fun game.

One day, we met a girl named Esther there. She was 11 years old and full of life. Even though she was sick, she had the brightest smile. She told funny jokes, loved reading comic books, and had a laugh that made you laugh along with her. She had something called sickle cell anemia, which made her feel tired or in pain sometimes. But just as Paul said, "Rejoice in the Lord always" (Philippians 4:4), Esther maintained her joy regardless of the circumstances.

Esther had to visit the hospital every month. Sometimes she stayed for several days at a time. Her birthday was approaching, so my mother discussed with her parents how we could make it special. We learned that Esther loved reading and laughing, so we brought her books and toys to share. *"It is more blessed to give than to receive"* (Acts 20:35), and that day, we felt that blessing in our hearts.

Her illness will require a long time to recover from. She will need the support of her doctors, nurses, parents, and friends every step of the way. Watching her made me think, *"What if I became a doctor one day?"* Or *maybe a nurse?* Or *even someone who donates money to help*

Children like Esther. "Each of you should use whatever gift you have received to serve others, as faithful stewards of God's grace in its various forms." (1 Peter 4:10), because God can use anyone to help.

Helping others is about more than just giving medicine. Some people choose to donate money, send thoughtful gifts, or visit to chat and bring smiles to kids. *Did*

you know some grandmas and grandpas team up with their trained dogs to brighten the day of children? That's precisely what Jesus appreciates, helpers with big, caring hearts. *"Let us not love with words or speech, but with actions and in truth"* (1 John 3:18). Every small act of kindness truly reflects God's love.

Many children around the world, like Esther, need love, kindness, and care. Some are in hospitals, others are at home, but all require compassion. Jesus said, *"Whatever you did for one of the least of these brothers and sisters of mine, you did for me".* When we help someone, it's like assisting Jesus to Himself.

So, *what about you?* What will you be when you grow up? A doctor, a teacher, a helper, or maybe a friend who makes others smile? The world needs more helpers with big hearts, just like you. *"Let your light shine before others, that they may see your good deeds and glorify your Father in heaven."* You and all of us belong to the kingdom of heaven.

My brother wished to commemorate the visit; he conducted inquiries, interviewed individuals, and compiled a list of medical and support professionals who assist children with sickle cell disorder:

- **Pediatrician:** A doctor who helps children with overall health.
- **Hematologist:** A blood specialist who specializes in understanding sickle cell disease.
- **Nurse:** Assists with daily care and administering medications.
- **Nurse Aide:** Assists nurses in caring for the child.
- **Child Life Specialist:** Helps children feel comfortable and happy in hospitals.
- **Psychologist:** Supports the child's emotions and feelings.
- **Social Worker:** Helps families find support and resources for payment
- **Pharmacist:** Gives the right medicine and explains how to use it.
- **Physical Therapist:** Helps the child move and stay strong.
- **Nutritionist:** Ensures the child eats a healthy diet for energy and healing.
- **School Tutor:** Helps the child keep learning even when in the hospital.
- **Hospital Pastor:** Prays and encourages the family with God's Word.
- **Occupational Therapist:** Helps with everyday tasks the child may struggle with.
- **Genetic Counsellor:** Educates families about the disorder and guides future planning.

- **Volunteers**: Bring toys, games, and smiles to children during their stay.
- **Donors and Sponsors**: Provide financial support or supplies to help cover the costs of care.

On our way back home, Gershom and Isaiah used only the letters from A to P (*A, B, C, D, E, F, G, H, I, J, K, L, M, N, O, P*) to explore and discover medical terms and anatomy-related words. It became a fun and educational challenge as we searched for real terms that could be formed without using any other letters beyond P.

Would you like to be included? Please let us know if we have missed any words.

Body Parts, Anatomy, Medical Terms, Tools, and Conditions

Abdomen, bile, bone, ear, eye, face, fibula, hand, hip, jaw, knee, labia, lobe, limb, lung, palm. Anemia, coma, cold, edema, gland, lab, lobe, pain, panic, bandage, bedpan, clip, exam, lamp, pad, pen, pill, pin.

Chapter Fifteen

Millions of Children have never heard of Jesus

Do you know any kids who've never heard about our Lord Jesus Christ?

HEAVENLY CITIZEN

*Let's share His love with the children
who haven't yet heard it.*

Millions of children around the world have never heard of Jesus. **Just imagine! So many boys and girls like you have never heard of the greatest Friend who ever lived.** They have never heard about His love for them, His sacrifice for them, or His desire to walk with them every day. That's why this message is essential; someone like you can help share this fantastic news with your friends and family.

Do you know any kids who've never heard about our Lord Jesus Christ?

Perhaps in your neighborhood, at school, or in the places you hang out, some kids are unaware of who Jesus is. It's not their fault. No one has told them about Him. **But you can now be the one to change that and tell them.** Jesus loves using children like you to share His love with others in quiet and beautiful ways, by being kind, telling stories, or praying for friends who don't know Him yet.

Now is the time! If you don't know enough about Jesus to tell others, **ask your mommy or daddy what they know.** They'll help you understand, and then you'll be able to share the good news too.

What about you? Do you know enough stories of Jesus to

Share with others?

If so, that's wonderful! If not, don't worry, you're teaching it now. Jesus knows you and made sure you found this message. You're not here by chance. *Whether your family takes you to church, mosque, or nowhere, Jesus wants you to know that He sees you, hears you, and loves you more than anyone else ever could.*

Perhaps you attend church and have already heard stories about Jesus. That's wonderful! Or maybe you come from a different background and have never really heard about him. *That's okay.* Jesus welcomes everyone, no matter where they come from or what they look like.

And he wants to be your friend, forever. This letter, written with love, is from Jesus, for you. *Yes, you! Right here, right now, you are his new best friend.*

You are a very special child. Your family is special, too. Your friends are special as well. You now have something more precious: the truth about Jesus. And Jesus wants you to share that love. He wants you to pass on this message as a gift. Perhaps you could say to your friend, brother, sister, or even your parents, "Jesus loves you." That simple phrase could change their whole life.

Jesus said:

"Hello, my child. You are now my friend. My name is Jesus."

Isn't it amazing that we're friends? The Son of God, the Savior of the world, wants to be your friend! I am not far away. I am always very close to you. I am right beside you right now, as you read these words. I know your name, your favorite games, your favorite colors, and even your most secret thoughts. And today, I am saying to you, "You are my special friend forever." You are loved, you are strong, you are kind and full of life, you are intelligent, you are wonderfully made, you are my amazing friend. From now on, no one can separate you from my love; our friendship will last forever.

From Jesus, your best friend.

"*I am all-knowing*," Jesus said. That means He knows everything: **your past, your present, and your future.** "I know what makes you laugh, and what makes you cry. I know your dreams, your fears, and your secrets". **And guess what?** "My love for you is deeper than anyone else's love could ever be. That's what makes me such a good friend. You can tell me anything, anytime."

Whenever you feel sad, scared, or confused, Jesus says to you, "*Come to me, my child.*" You don't need fancy words to pray to me. You don't need a microphone, to speak loudly, or a stage. Just talk to Jesus like you would talk to a friend beside you. Whisper if you need to, from your heart. Shout if you want to, if you're alone. He listens to you every time. *He hears every prayer of children.* And what's more important, *he promises to answer.* He will help you, support you, and heal your heart.

Jesus proved His love in the most extraordinary way possible. He died on the cross, taking the sins of the world with Him, including yours. But he didn't stay dead. Three days later, *He came back to life!* Why? To show that nothing, not even death, could stop His love for you. That's what makes Jesus different from everyone else. He's not just a friend; He's the Savior. "*When you ask for something in My name, I will do it.* This shows how great God is.

If you ask Me for anything because you believe in Me, I will do it for you." John 14:13-14: *I am telling you again, my child, "You may ask me for anything in my name, and I will do it.*

Jesus rejoices with you. When you're nervous, He brings you peace. He never forsakes you, never forgets you, and never gives up on you. Jesus is always by your side. All you need to do is keep your faith in him.

Now it's up to you. *Will you believe in this Jesus, who loves you so much? Will you be His friend too? All you have to do is talk to Him. Say to Him, "**Jesus, I believe in You. I want to be your friend forever.**" And then go and tell others, because there are still millions of children around the world who have not yet heard about Him. But they will listen to Him thanks to you. Because of your message, they'll become Christians and friends with Jesus.*

Jesus said to all his friends: "**Be strong and brave. Don't be afraid. The Lord your God will go before you. He will not leave you or forget you.**"

No child can hide from Jesus! **Did you know that?** King David said:

"Where can I go to get away from Your Spirit? Where can I run from You?

If I go up to the heavens, you are there.

If I go down to the deepest place, you are there too. If I rise with the sun in the east or live far away in the

west, even there, you will take my hand and hold me."
(Psalm 139:7 10)

The Lord Jesus wishes to communicate that His presence accompanies you wherever your endeavors take you, whether it be to school, home, the playground, or your bed at night. In moments of loneliness or excitement, He rejoices alongside you. When you experience nervousness, He grants you peace. He remains unwaveringly by your side, never forgetting you, and never abandoning you. **Jesus will always stand with you consistently.**

Diane's Story

One day, I asked my friend Diane why she didn't believe in Jesus. She looked at me for a moment and then said, "When I was a kid, my parents used to take me to church. However, now that I am older, I no longer see the point. I don't think it's real."

Her answer made me sad, but it also gave me courage. You see, I didn't have to answer her alone. I had the Lord with me, and I also had my little brother Gershom. He is younger than me, but sometimes God uses the youngest voices to speak the loudest truth.

King David says, *"Out of the mouths of children and infants you have ordained praise"* (Psalm 8:2). And that day, Gershom was ready to preach.

Gershom Explains

Gershom looked at Diane with a big smile. Then he asked her, "**Do you believe in darkness?**"

Diane nodded. "**Yes**, of course."

"**Are you afraid of darkness?**" he continued.

"**Yes**, who doesn't!" Diane said again.

"**Great!**" Gershom replied. "Now, what would make your life better in the darkness?"

Diane thought for a second and said, "**The light.**"

"**Amazing**," Gershom said, his eyes shining. "**Guess what?** Jesus is **the light!**"

Then Gershom opened his little Bible and read: *"I am the light of the world. Whoever follows me will not walk in darkness, but will have the light of life"* (John 8:12).

At that moment, something powerful happened. Diane didn't laugh or roll her eyes. She stopped and listened.

She thought about what Gershom had said.

My little preacher said, "**Seeing What We Cannot See**"

Gershom went on to explain, "You can't see electricity flowing through the wires. But when you flip the switch, the light turns on. You know it's there because you see the effect of it."

"**It's the same way with Jesus**," he continued. "You may not see Him standing right in front of you, but you can see the effects of His presence in people's lives. You see it when someone is healed. You see it when someone forgives. You see it when families come together in love.

That's Jesus at work."

You will undoubtedly see Jesus whenever you can breathe independently, your brain remains functional, you go out and return safely, and you experience death in your dreams and awaken from sleeping every day. As my father used to say, **every day is a blessing.** He allowed you to wake up so that you could believe and make wise choices.

One of the most brilliant scholars, Paul, said: *"Now faith is confidence in what we hope for and assurance about what we do not see"* (Hebrews 11:1). Faith means trusting in God even when our eyes cannot see Him.

Why do we believe in Jesus? Someone asked.

In our family, we often talk about Jesus. We believe He is real, not just because we read about Him, but because we see Him working in our lives every single day.

When we pray, He responds. When we are scared, He gives us peace. When we mess up, He forgives us. That's how we know He is alive.

The Bible says: **"Taste and see that the Lord is good; blessed is the one who takes refuge in him"** (Psalm 34:8). Believing in Jesus is like tasting something sweet and wanting more. Once you experience His love, you can't deny that He is real.

We are the Children of the Living Christ

We are not only children of our parents; we are children of the living Christ. That means we belong to God's family. **We are citizens of His heavenly Kingdom, and our home is with Him forever.**

The Apostle John wrote: *"See what great love the Father has lavished on us, that we should be called children of God! And that is what we are!"* (1 John 3:1).

Being God's child gives us an identity that the world cannot take away. Even if people laugh at us or say Jesus isn't honest, we know the truth. We walk in the light, and the light cannot be overcome by darkness (John 1:5).

The Door Is Open

At the end of the conversation, Gershom said something I will never forget: **"Diane,** the door is wide open for you. You can choose to believe in Jesus today. He is inviting you to be His friend."

That is true for every child, teenager, and adult worldwide. Jesus never forces us to follow Him. He offers us the choice. But He also promises: "Here I am! I stand at the door and knock. If anyone hears my voice and opens the door, I will come in and eat with that person, and they with me" (Revelation 3:20).

The door is open. The choice is ours.

A Question for You:

Now I want to ask you: do you know people like Diane? Maybe some of your friends don't believe in Jesus. Perhaps even someone in your family says they don't see the point. That might not feel very encouraging, but don't give up.

You don't have to argue or fight. You can do **what Gershom did**: share the truth with love, using simple words and examples. You can also pray for your friends, asking God to open their hearts and minds.

The Bible says: "Always be prepared to answer everyone who asks you to give the reason for the hope that you have. But do this with gentleness and respect" (1 Peter 3:15). That means we can tell others about Jesus without being mean or proud. We share the truth and let God handle the rest.

My Choice, Your Choice

I have made my choice. I choose to follow Jesus. I prefer to be His friend. I decide to walk in the light instead of the darkness.

What about you?

Being a friend of Jesus doesn't mean life will always be easy. Sometimes people might not understand us, and we'll face challenges. But Jesus promised to be with us always, even until the very end (Matthew 28:20). That makes me brave.

When you choose Jesus, you gain a friend who never abandons you, a Savior who forgives, and a King who welcomes you into His everlasting Kingdom.

I am a child. But I am also a friend of Jesus. And that makes me strong. My family has chosen to follow Him, and together we shine His light. But the best part is this: you don't have to be left out. The door is open for you, too.

Remember His words: *"I am the light of the world. Whoever follows me will not walk in darkness, but will have the light of life"* (John 8:12). So come, step into the light. Be a friend of Jesus. You will never regret it.

A Prayer for My Friends

Dear Lord Jesus,

Thank you for being my best friend and always being there for me. You are the light of the world, and you shine in my heart every day.

Today, I want to pray for my friends who do not yet know You. Some of them, like my friend Diane, do not believe because they cannot see You. Please open their hearts and help them see Your love through the way I live, speak, and share kindness.

Give me the courage to tell them about You with kindness and respect. Let my words be truthful, and let my actions reflect Your light.

Lord, protect my friends from walking in darkness. Show them that You are real and that Your love never ends. Just as Gershom explained that light is stronger than darkness, help my friends discover that You are the Light that gives life.

I pray for every child in the world who feels unsure about You. May they find peace in Your presence and joy in being part of Your family.

Thank you for hearing my prayer. I trust you, Jesus, and I believe that one day my friends will also become Your friends. In Your holy name I pray, Amen.

Chapter Sixteen

My cousin's name is Olivia F.
A friend of Jesus

Do you know the meaning of your name?

HEAVENLY CITIZEN

Do you know the meaning of your name?

My cousin's name is **Olivia**. She is one of my closest friends, and *guess what*? She also happens to be a friend of Jesus. *Olivia has a smile that lights up a room and a laugh that spreads happiness to everyone.* But what makes her story so special is how she came into this world and how much Jesus has been with her from the very beginning.

Olivia was born two months earlier than expected, which required her mother to have a special surgery called a C-section. She arrived after only seven months in her mother's belly, perhaps in a joyful rush to meet her family. We like to imagine that she couldn't wait to meet her father, who was the greatest dad in the world.

Her name, **Olivia,** *comes from the word "olive tree," a symbol of peace, blessing, and life. In the Bible, the olive tree is a sign of enduring strength, as it can live for hundreds of years while continuing to bear fruit.*

When Olivia was born, she was tiny and had to stay in the hospital for two whole months before she could finally go home. During that time, the doctors and nurses cared for her with great skill and kindness. But above all, the most important one watching over her was Jesus, who held her in His love from the very beginning.

She had a condition called **respiratory distress syndrome**, which means her lungs weren't ready to function on their own. So, Olivia needed a tube in her nose to help her breathe. Her lungs were still developing because she was born very early, so her tiny lungs didn't have something called surfactant, which is like a soft bubble that helps her lungs stay open, allowing her to breathe.

Her body was also tiny, and she didn't have enough baby fat yet to keep herself warm, like a blanket on a cold day. The doctors had to help her stay warm and feed her through a tube, because she couldn't suck or swallow food yet. She couldn't eat regular food for a long time. That made me a little sad, but we all continued to pray, and we knew Jesus was helping her grow stronger every day.

Do you know any children with difficulties?

How does that make you feel?

Some children born prematurely have a difficult time learning certain things. But Jesus was the best friend to our family. He helped my aunt and uncle stay strong. Their names are Croilnor and Hannah, like the mother of King Samuel in the bible.

He provided them with hope, peace, and joy during challenging times. He was consistently present with my cousin *Olivia*, even as she slept in her small hospital bed, encircled by tubes and machines. Jesus was there by her side. Now, Olivia is 100% healthy! *Isn't that amazing*? She can run, play, and read just like any other kid. She tells the funniest jokes and loves reading comic books. She says that:

"*When you are a friend of Jesus, life becomes an adventure*".

You find joy even in the most challenging times. And guess what? She was right! Olivia reminds me a lot of our friend Esther from the Children's Hospital in Massachusetts. Olivia and Esther share many similarities: they both had difficult beginnings, and they both have big hearts full of faith in Jesus. **"Faith means trusting God for what we hope will happen. It means believing, even when we can't see it yet."** Hebrews 11:1

I'm sure you would love my cousin, Olivia, and my friend, Esther, if you ever had the chance to meet them. They are amazing, kind, and full of joy. They understand what it means to be strong and never give up, because Jesus is "**Jehovah Rapha**," the Lord who heals, with them every step of the way.

So, if you ever feel alone or have a friend or family member who is sick or going through a tough time, remember the stories of Olivia and Esther. Remember how Jesus will never leave or forsake you. Jesus is the best friend anyone could ever have. Just like He helped Olivia and Esther, He will help you as well. All you need to do is believe and talk to Him in prayer, because He's always listening.

Now, your turn. *Can you find out how many times Jesus said, "Follow me."*

Jesus said, "Follow me and be kind."

One sunny day, my big brother Gabe was out playing with his friends when he noticed a new kid sitting alone on the playground. It made him think of something his Sunday school teacher once told him: "*Jesus wants us to follow him by being kind.*" Feeling inspired, Gabe went over with a warm smile and asked, '*Do you want to play with us*?' The boy's face instantly brightened with happiness. That wonderful day, Gabe not only gained a new friend but also chose to follow Jesus with love. His name was Frederick. When we choose to live like Jesus, we help others feel special, seen, and loved.

God loves children! There was a little girl named Myriam who loved singing for Jesus every night. Her name means *Beloved and gentle soul*. Although she didn't always understand the complex words in the Bible, her heart was filled with love and trust. One day, her grandmother said to her, "*Myriam, the Bible says children are a gift from God, you are my gift, I love you*!" She smiled and said, "*I love you too,*

Grandma!" Jesus observes the hearts of children, and even as they grow older, they will continue to love with childlike affection.

God Guides Myriam and Her Grandma to Help

A True Story About Listening to the Holy Spirit, inspired by Romans 8:14: "For all who the Spirit of God leads are children of God."

Myriam's grandmother, Ms. Edna, was not just her grandma; she was also a close friend of Jesus. Myriam loved going to church with her every Sunday, and afterward, they always shared a special lunch. They loved good food.

Myriam's favorite place to eat was a restaurant called **"The Legal Sea Foods,"** and that's precisely where they were supposed to go that evening.

But **"NOOO"** as Ms. Edna started driving, she suddenly felt something gentle in her heart, something she recognized as the Holy Spirit whispering, **"Go somewhere else today."**

Ms. Edna turned to Myriam and said, "Sweetheart, we're going to a different restaurant today. Jesus is leading us to *"Ocean Prime instead."* She was a little surprised, but she knew her grandma always listened to Jesus. Myriam asked if she could get steak and fries there, and she said, *"Oh yes, they have it best".*

They arrived at **Ocean Prime** and enjoyed their meal, laughter, and a conversation about their church day. Just as they were about to finish eating, they heard a loud commotion at a nearby table. *A young girl was choking and unable to breathe.* Her face became red, her eyes widened with fear, and she clutched her small hands around her throat.

Her dad, who was a senator, shouted, "Call an ambulance!" Her mother cried out in panic, unsure of what to do. People stood frozen, afraid and confused. No one knew what to do.

But not Ms. Edna.

She hurried over, carefully picked up the little girl, and tilted her forward. Kneeling behind her, she wrapped one arm around the girl's waist, made a fist, and placed it just above her belly button. With her other hand, she grabbed the fist and gave firm, upward thrusts. Then she began counting:

One... two... three...

On the fourth thrust, the piece of food flew out! The girl gasped and started to breathe again. Everyone in the restaurant clapped and cried tears of relief.

The parents hugged their daughter tightly, then turned to Ms. Edna and Myriam in amazement. "Thank you! Thank you so much!" they said, full of gratitude.

But Ms. Edna smiled gently and replied, "Don't thank me. Thank Jesus. He told me to come here today, instead of our usual restaurant. He is the one who saved your daughter."

As they left the restaurant, Myriam looked up at her grandma and whispered, "*Grandma, why didn't you tell them you're a nurse?*"

Ms. Edna smiled again and said, "*Because the glory doesn't belong to me. It all belongs to Jesus.*"

My family serves the Lord Jesus Christ. Gabe, Gershom, and Isaiah's family is a large, loving, and caring family. Every Saturday, they pick up trash in the park and distribute cookies and drinks to their neighbors. *Their father always says, "As for me and my house, we will serve the Lord!"* Gershom and his brothers obey their parents joyfully, and Mom and Dad listen to them with love and patience. When families work together to follow God, their home becomes a place filled with joy, peace, and a sense of unity.

God has a great plan!

Jesus Is Our Shepherd: God Has a Great Plan!

Uncle Jean once found himself lost, not just physically, but also in the passage of time and the ups and downs of life. He felt scared, unsure of where to go, and the loneliness weighed heavily on his heart.

Then he remembered a Bible verse that King David once spoke when he was in trouble: "The Lord is my Shepherd. I will not be afraid." *Along with these words, Jean recalled the promise of Jesus in* John 10:14: *"I am the good shepherd; I know my sheep and my sheep know me."* These verses reminded him that even when life feels uncertain, he belongs to a Shepherd who knows his name and cares deeply for him.

The first time my Uncle Jean met Gabe, Isaiah, and Gershom, he stood quietly, unsure how to behave around them. Their well-mannered speech and deep respect for others were immediately evident. After a few moments, Gershom asked him gently, *"Do you know the Lord Jesus Christ?"* Uncle Jean replied, *"Not really."* Gershom smiled and said, *"Would you like me to teach you about Jesus, the greatest friend who has ever lived?"* Jean nodded, **"Yes"**.

Gershom continued, *"Have you heard about a book called the Bible?"* Jean answered, "Yes." "Do you own one"? *"No"*. Gershom explained, "The Bible is made up of 66 books, divided into two parts: the Old Testament and the New Testament. It tells the story of God's love for us and how Jesus came to save us. Jesus said in John 14:6, *'I am the way, the truth, and the life. No one comes to the father except through Me.'"* Then he asked, *"If you were to die today, do you know where you would go?* There are only two destinations: heaven or eternal separation from God's kingdom. *Which one will you choose?"*

Gershom explained, "Romans 10:9 says, *'If you confess with your mouth, "Jesus is Lord," and believe in your heart that God raised Him from the dead, you will be saved.'* This isn't difficult to understand; it's so simple that many people reject it. But now you know the truth. *You can accept Jesus as your Lord and Savior today."*

Uncle Jean looked at the three brothers and said, *"I accept Jesus and want to become a Christian."* The three brothers prayed for him, and in that moment, *Uncle Jean was saved*, just as Jesus promised in John 10:28: *"I give them eternal life, and they shall never perish; no one will snatch them out of My hand.*"

Just as a good shepherd never leaves a lost sheep, Jesus will always stay with us. He walks alongside, guides our steps, and shields us from harm, even when we cannot see Him at work. Jesus says, "*I know you by name, you are Mine*" (Isaiah 43:1). Uncle Jean realized he was never truly alone; the Good Shepherd was always nearby, ready to lead him back to safety. At that moment, his fear started to fade, replaced by the comforting warmth of God's presence. He understood that no matter how lost he might feel in life, *Jesus' love and care would always find him and bring him home.*

Here's something amazing: *because you are a child, God can use you to save adults!* Many adults have never truly taken the time to understand the love of Jesus or how to be saved. Most people believe that living a "good life" is sufficient to gain entry to heaven. *But as Gershom showed Uncle Jean, the Bible teaches otherwise.* "*For all have sinned and fall short of the glory of God*" (Romans 3:23), and "the gift of God is eternal life in Christ Jesus our Lord" (Romans 6:23). It was through Gershom's simple, loving explanation of the gospel that *Uncle Jean learned the truth*, and that day, *he found the Good Shepherd for himself.*

The Bible is a very special book for children.

There's a special book that has been loved by millions of children for thousands of years. *This book is known as the Bible, and it is one of the most influential* books in the world. We will tell you all about it here. *Just keep reading.*

If something is the most expensive in the world and could save the lives of billions of people, *would you agree you'd want to own it or have access to it*? Your answer is "**Yes**," of course. What about if it's a book full of *secrets: Healing every single disease on the planet earth and the Broken-hearted, Bringing True Peace, Saving Lives for Eternity, Breaking Chains of Sin and Addiction, Guiding Our Steps, Protecting from Spiritual Dangers, Transforming the Mind, and Bringing Joy and Hope?*

The three brothers are: Gabe is 12 years old; Isaiah is 9, and Gershom is 7. They answered this question, too. They all said, "**Yes**! We would want to own it and even buy it, especially if it were hard to get. *That would make it even more valuable!*" One of the brothers said he would share pages with friends who couldn't afford it. Most people would be curious to read it and learn the rules for living from such an important book, right?

Well, here's the amazing part: **the Bible is free!** Not because nobody cares, but because the One it teaches about, "Jesus," was rejected by many people, except us, the children of God's Kingdom. *That's why it's so essential for children to take time to read the Bible*, so we can understand who Jesus is and how to live for Him.

Chapter Seventeen

The Bible is a Big Library of God's Love

The Old Testament library: **39 Books**
The New Testament: **27 Books**

HEAVENLY CITIZEN

The Bible
The Bible has two main parts:
the Old Testament and the New Testament.

The Old Testament was written a long time ago, approximately between 1400 and 1200 BCE, and it describes the stories of God's people from the start of the world.

The first five books: Genesis, Exodus, Leviticus, Numbers, and Deuteronomy, were written by Moses. He helped God's people, the Israelites, follow God's rules and Jesus' laws that guide them to live as He wanted. A very good man of God. And his eldest son had the same name as my little brother, "**Gershom**." Can you tell your parent *what this name means? Make your research....*

The New Testament was written roughly 1,900 to 2,000 years ago. It recounts the story of Jesus, *who came to teach us how to love one another and serve God with all our hearts and minds.* It also describes how His followers, like Peter, Paul, and other friends, spread the good news of Jesus around the world.

The New Testament was written over about 50 years, and it teaches us how to live as God's children and Jesus' friends. The Bible is unique among other books because it is a collection of different writings.

66 books to be exact! More than 40 different people wrote these books over **about 1,500 years** in **three different languages: Hebrew, Aramaic**, and **Greek**.

But even though many people wrote it, the Bible tells one story: **God's love for us and His plan for saving us through Jesus Christ**.

The Bible is also the most read and most popular book ever in the world! No other book has been read by so many people or for such a long time. Jesus and King David are the two names mentioned most often in the

Bible. *Jesus' name is mentioned almost 1,000 times, and King David's name is mentioned over 1,000 times, too!*

The Big Library of God's Love

And His Instructions for His Children

One bright afternoon, little Gabriel and his sister Angie quietly entered their grandmother's warm living room. The scent of vanilla cookies and old books filled the air. Sunlight streamed through the window, illuminating an object placed at the center of the coffee table. It was a **big, thick book with a shiny cover.**

Gabriel's eyes grew wide. *"What's that, Grandma?"*

Grandma looked up from her knitting, her face glowing with a

Gentle smile. "This, my dear, is the **Bible**. It's not just a book. It's like a **giant library** all inside one cover, filled with adventures, poems, songs, letters, and even secret instructions from God Himself. And **guess what**? It has two big sections."

Angie tilted her head. "Like two sides of a treasure chest?"

"**Yes**," Grandma chuckled softly. "Exactly like that."

She gently rested her hand on the cover. "After people sinned and separated themselves from God, He was still too pure and too powerful for us to stand before Him. But because He loves us so much, He provided a guidebook for life and survival, this **Bible**. Every page offers wisdom for us to find our way back to Him, to His kingdom."

The Old Testament of the Lord's library: 39 Books

Grandma opened the first half of the **Bible**, and the old pages crackled like a whisper. Angie frowned slightly. "But Grandma, I'm not a good reader."

Grandma raised an eyebrow. "You mean you don't read well?"

Angie nodded shyly. "Yes. What's the difference?"

Grandma put her arm around her. "**Sweetheart,** with the Lord, you don't have to read like everyone else. Even if you read slowly or silently, He listens. You don't need to memorize every word because the Holy Spirit will guide you with what you need."

"**Really?**" Angie whispered.

"Really," Grandma said. Then she leaned in closer and playfully winked. "**Close your eyes.** I'll show you an example of God's wisdom."

So, Angie squeezed her eyes shut. The room was silent and calming.

Now tell me," Grandma said, "what is the color of the big house next to 1000 Canal Street, Brooklyn, New York?" Angie scrunched her face. "**I don't know!**"

Grandma laughed softly. "And that's the point! We don't know everything. That's why God gave us this **Bible**, like a GPS to His

Heavenly Kingdom. Everyone is free to choose whether to go there, but the path is clear: you need to believe in the Lord with all your heart, mind, and strength. That is the greatest commandment."

Mark 12:30:

"Love the Lord your God with all your heart and with all your soul and with all your mind and with all your strength."

Angie opened her eyes and whispered, "**Wow**... it really is like a map."

Grandma nodded. "**Yes**. And the first part of this map is called the **Old Testament**. It has **thirty-nine books**. These tell the stories of how God created the world, how He chose people like **Abraham, Moses, David, and Solomon**, and how prophets spoke God's messages."

Gabriel leaned closer. "Wait, prophets? Like who?"

Grandma's eyes twinkled. "Prophets like **Isaiah** and **Jeremiah**. And do you know who delivered God's messages to them? An angel named **Gabriel**, just like you!"

Gabriel's chest puffed out. "**Really?**"

"**Oh yes**," Grandma said. "Gabriel is one of God's most trusted messengers. When he flies, it's like a mighty earthquake shakes the heavens, and winds roar with power. He is a protector of God's people. Because of angels like him, we have these instructions that tell us to hold on to our faith." Angie giggled. "So, he's like a **hero**?"

"**Exactly!**" Grandma replied. "The Old Testament is filled with **heroes, kings, and brave women** like Ruth and Esther. They all pointed to something significant that was coming... someone very special."

Grandma paused and whispered, "**That someone is the Lord**

Jesus Christ."

She closed the book for a moment and held it to her heart. "Jesus came from heaven to save us all. But my dear children, many people never read the library God gave us. And when they don't read it, they get lost. None of us can find heaven on our own; we need the Lord to guide us."

Gabriel and Angie sat quietly, their little hearts pounding with curiosity.

The New Testament: 27 Books

Grandma opened the second half of the Bible. The pages looked newer, like a fresh chapter waiting to be discovered.

"These are the **27 books of the New Testament**," Grandma explained. "This part tells the **truth of Jesus, the Son of God.** It shows how He came to earth to reveal God's love in the clearest, most powerful way."

Gabriel whispered, "So... Jesus is the most important story, right?"

"**Exactly**," Grandma said warmly. "Here, we read about His birth in Bethlehem, His miracles that healed the sick and fed the hungry, His death on the cross, and His resurrection three days later. Then we read about His followers, like Peter, Paul, and John, who went everywhere teaching others how to live in His love."

Angie's face lit up. "**So that's how we belong to His kingdom in heaven!**"

"Yes, Angie," Grandma replied. "The New Testament shows us how to be saved and how to walk in the light of Jesus."

The Heart of the Story

Grandma reached for her glasses and carefully read aloud from the book of John:

"*Jesus said, 'I give you a new command: Love one another.*

Just as I have loved you, you should love each other.' (John 13:34)"

Angie's eyes sparkled. "So, the whole Bible is about learning to love God and love others?"

Grandma pulled both children close into her arms. "That's right, my loves. The Bible is like a giant library, but every single page points to the greatest story of all, **God's love through Jesus.**" **1 John 4:8:**

"*Whoever does not love does not know God, because God is love.*"

She kissed their foreheads and whispered, "Jesus is life. He is the bread of life. He is our only way to God's kingdom."

Gabriel's grin stretched from ear to ear. "That makes this the **best book ever!**"

Grandma laughed. "Yes, my child. Every page is more valuable than the biggest scientific research, more than the most advanced medicine, more than the greatest university lessons. It comes directly from the Lord to all of us."

"Children," she said, "this book has many parts, Genesis and Exodus, Psalms and Proverbs, Matthew and John, Revelation and more. But together, they all weave one great truth: **God loves us and calls us to love others.**"

Angie hugged her grandma tightly. "I want to read it, even if I'm not the best reader."

"And I want to be like the angel Gabriel, strong and faithful," said Gabriel.

Grandma's eyes grew misty with joy. "That is exactly what God wants, for you to read His Word, to trust His Spirit, and to shine His love wherever you go."

Outside, the first stars began to twinkle. Grandma whispered one last time, "Remember, my little ones: **the Bible is the Big Library of God's Love and His instructions for His children.** Whenever you open it, you are never lost, you are always finding your way home."

The Bible contains many books and different kinds of stories, but together they form one great treasure: God's unending love. Through the Old Testament and the New Testament, through heroes, kings, prophets, and Jesus Himself, we learn how to love God, how to love others, and how to live as God's beloved children.

The Bible may be an old book, but it still holds wisdom and love that can guide us every day. And remember, **no matter your age,** God's Word is always there to teach, guide you, and help you live your best life!

A Prayer for Every Child Who Reads This Book

Dear Jesus,
Thank you for your letter. I love you too.
Thank you for loving me and my family.
Thank you for being our forever friend.
Help me always follow You, to be kind, gentle, and full of love.
Teach me to forgive, share, and care for others.
Bless my mommy, daddy, brothers, sisters, and all of my friends.
Fill my heart with Your joy and peace every day.
Let my family shine with Your light, and help us always walk close to You.
Please keep our family and our home safe and happy. In your name, I pray. Amen.

Who is Jesus?

Have you ever wondered, "**Who is Jesus?**" Was he just a prophet, like those who came before him, given a divine task to save humanity?

Remember: Christian children *are very skilled at critical thinking.* Reread the question. *Can you spot something unusual?*

"*Yes*, Jesus Was Someone Who Came

The Bible mentions many times that Jesus came, "**You say that I am a king. In fact, the reason I was born and came into the world is to testify to the truth. Everyone on the side of truth listens to me.**" (John 18:37 "*Here is a trustworthy saying that deserves full acceptance*" (1 Timothy 1:15): Christ Jesus came into the world to save sinners. But why does it say *came instead of was born*, like everyone else? That's because Jesus didn't start His life as a baby. **What, how?**

He already existed before He came to earth! Through him all things were made; without him nothing was made that has been made. In him was life, and that life was **the light of all humanity.**

John 1:3-5:

The light shines in the darkness, and the darkness has not overcome it. Who was His real Father? His Father is God in Heaven: One day, an angel called "Gabriel » came to Mary with excellent news:

"Mary, you are going to have a very special baby! He will be great and will be called the Son of the Most-High God. God will give Him the throne of King David, and He will be the King forever, His kingdom will never end!"

Mary was surprised and asked, "But how can this happen? I'm not even married yet."

The angel said, "The Holy Spirit will come to you, and God's power will cover you like a shadow. That's why the baby you will have will be holy, and He will be called the Son of God. Even your cousin Elizabeth, who is very old and couldn't have children, is now six months pregnant! Nothing is impossible for God."

Now we have two cousins: one was young and unmarried, and the other was unable to have children. Yet both received incredible news that no human mind could fully comprehend. Mary was chosen to give birth to Jesus through the power of the Holy Spirit, and Elizabeth was blessed with John the Baptist, the very one who would later baptize Jesus in the Jordan River. Do you see what this means? Every detail was perfectly planned and arranged by God, demonstrating that nothing is impossible for Him (Luke 1:32-37).

That's why He could do things no one else could. For example, even though He never went to school, Jesus could read the scrolls of the prophets (Luke 4:16-21). He even knew people's thoughts without them saying a word (Matthew 9:46). Jesus had authority on earth to forgive sins, which is something only God can do!

Without sins, we would live here on earth forever, right?

Remember: Christian children have excellent **critical thinking skills** to ask and answer good, complex questions!

Jesus said, **"I am the Life. My name is I AM, and you are Mine."** These are not ordinary words. **"I AM"** is the very name God used when He spoke to Moses from the burning bush (Exodus 3:14). By calling Himself **"I AM,"** Jesus was not just claiming to have God's attributes; He was declaring that **He is God Himself.**

His words reveal His divine identity, the One **who gives life**, who owns

us, and who has no beginning or end. Not one person can be saved except through him (John 14:6; **"I and the Father are one»** which means if you see him, you see the Father (John 10:30).

Jesus said He was alive before the world was made and that **everything was created through Him and for Him** (John 17:5; Colossians 1:16). So, who was He? He was, and still is, **the Son of God, the Savior of the world** (John 3:16).

He didn't just come to live here; He came to rescue us and bring us back to God.

Jesus said, "**Since I came, died, and shed my blood for you, you will no longer die, as you are like the angels. My blood saves you, and you are God's children because you are children of the resurrection.**" (Luke 20:36)

Do you have enough information to think for yourself about who Jesus is now?

Was Jesus just **a wise teacher** sharing king's stories, or a compassionate man helping people experiencing poverty because He cared? Could he be simply a character from an old story, or **is He real and alive today, still working in people's lives**? Did He only speak to adults, or did He also care about kids? Is He someone distant from the past, or **is He the Savior who knows your name and loves you more than anyone else**?

These questions matter greatly because the way we answer them influences how we live, what we hope for, and what we believe about forever.

Let's use our brains and think about this together! Let's ask the right question: **Do we believe there was a man named Albert Einstein?**

Yes, we do! So, **who was he?** He was a brilliant man in

history.

Albert Einstein was a super-smart scientist who helped everyone understand the universe in a whole new way. He discovered the **theory of relativity**, which explains how space, time, and gravity interact, and he formulated the famous equation $E = mc^2$, demonstrating the connection between energy and matter. But what made him famous to this day was his **curiosity, imagination, and love of learning**, just like Christian children who read this book! That same *curiosity and love for God's truth can make you one of the most intelligent children of God and a best friend of Jesus in the world*, just like Gabe, Isaiah, and Gershom.

Now, **think of it this way**: it's like believing in a real person named *Jesus*.

He was a boy born in a town called **Bethlehem**. He grew up with two parents, just like us, and had friends, just like we do.

But here's the fantastic part: **Jesus didn't have to attend school to learn, as** He was already **wise and gifted**. Smarter than anyone in the whole world, ever!

We are young believers, intelligent, and children of God

We may be young, but we are *smart too*, which means we can ask good questions, *be curious*, and use our *minds to learn* more about Jesus and all the amazing things He did.

So why is Jesus so special? Well, even now, in the year **2025**, more than **2.9 billion people** all over the world believe in Him!

Who are these people?

Children from all around the world follow Jesus, including both **rich** and **poor**, and many famous people like **Denzel** Washington, **Simone** Biles, **Chris** Pratt, and **Serena**.

Williams, and people of all ages. There are brilliant *scientists, artists, teachers, hardworking parents, students, and even kids like us who believe in Him.*

Some are pastors who teach about God, others are musicians, athletes, nurses, or builders, just regular people living their lives with faith. Teenagers finding their way, grandparents sharing wisdom, and **children full of questions and curiosity**. We all have a place in God's family and his heavenly kingdom.

You and I are alike. We are wonderfully created by God, with our talents, ideas, and dreams. And the best part is, we belong to the heavenly kingdom because we now believe in Jesus!

Chapter Eighteen

Where Did Jesus Come From?

Why Did Jesus Come?

HEAVENLY CITIZEN

Where Did Jesus Come From?

Jesus didn't start His life in Bethlehem; He originated from heaven! He has existed with God eternally, even before the creation of the world.

Proverbs 8:22-23: *"The Lord created me first, before He made anything else. I was there a long, long time ago, right at the very beginning, before the world was made.*

Jesus is God's Son, and He came to earth to help us, love us, and save us from sin. He didn't come just to visit; He went on a special mission.

Why Did Jesus Come?

Jesus came because He loves us so much. We had done wrong things called sin, which kept us away from God.

But we couldn't fix it on our own.

So, Jesus came to take the punishment for our sins and made a way for us to be close to God again. "The Son of Man came to look for the lost and save them." (Luke 19:10)

Was He Born Like You and Me?

Yes and no. Jesus was born as a baby, just like you and me, but He was exceptional. His mother was Mary, *but He didn't have a human father*. He was born a miracle, conceived through the power of the Holy Spirit!

"So, the baby will be holy and will be called the Son of God." Luke 1:35

Even though He had a body like ours, He possessed many powers.

What Did Jesus Think About Kids?

Jesus loved kids, just like you! He didn't ignore them or treat them as if they were too small. He said kids are an essential part of God's Kingdom.

Matthew 19:14

"Let the little children come to me... God's kingdom belongs to people like these."

Jesus listened to children, blessed them, and taught that their hearts are full of faith.

Do you have faith?

What does "**faith**" mean?

Well, since God made us smart, we can tell when something

Is it true or not?

Let's say you have a math problem: 17 + 17 - 6 =?

You work it out and believe your answer *is correct*. That's like having **faith**; you trust what you know is true.

But if you're not sure your answer is *correct*, you don't have *faith* in it.

As Christian kids, we believe Jesus is honest. Even though we can't see Him with our eyes, we trust Him with our hearts. That's what faith is: believing in Jesus and His love, even when we can't see Him.

And when we have that faith, we should share the good news with others!

Where Is Jesus Today?

After Jesus died on the cross and rose from the dead, He returned to heaven. Today, He sits beside God, watching over us, praying for us, and preparing a place for those who love Him.

"He was taken up into heaven... and sat at the right hand

of God." Mark 16:19

Why Should We Follow Jesus?

Because He's the only way to God, he's the truth, the light, the path to heaven, and the best friend you could ever have.

"I am the way, the truth, and the life. No one comes to the

Father accepts through me." John 14:6

Following Jesus teaches us to live like Him, with love, kindness, courage, and truth.

How Can I Follow Jesus?

You don't have to be perfect; you need to believe. Very simple.

Following Jesus means:

Jesus teaches us that being His friend means we don't always do what we want. Sometimes we have to make tough choices, like being kind when it's hard, sharing even when we don't want to, or doing what's right even when others aren't.

Jesus isn't just a figure from the past; He's alive today. He loves you. He sees you. He is calling you to walk with Him and to be his best friend.

Dear Jesus,
You are so **good and holy.**
May everyone know **You and your love.**
Let what you want be done.
Here on earth, just like it is in heaven.
I believe you are the Son of God.
I know I have done wrong sometimes, and I am sorry.
Thank you for loving me anyway.
Thank You for dying on the cross for my sins and coming back to life—today, and every day forever.
I ask you to enter my heart.
Be my Lord and Savior. Help me follow You and love You with all my heart. And trust You every day.
I want to live for You and share Your story with others.
Thank you for saving me, my parents, and my friends!
In Your name I pray, **Amen.**

John 14:9

"Anyone who has seen me has seen the father."

Let your light shine before others, so that they may see Jesus in you.

When you are a friend of Jesus, you represent Him everywhere you go, at school, at home, in the park, and even online, or when you travel to other countries. *The way you dress, speak, and act shows others what's in your heart.*

If your heart belongs to Jesus, you'll want to make Him proud. Just like a sports team wears matching uniforms to show they're on the same side, Christian's *"wear"* their faith by living and dressing in ways that honor Him.

Dressing up goes beyond simply wearing clothes; it's about expressing your personality and feeling confident both inside and out.

People can often judge you based on your appearance without knowing how wonderful you truly are inside. Would you agree?

The boys and girls of God resemble the angels in heaven to some extent. Gabriel functions as a messenger delivering significant messages from God, while Michael serves as a formidable leader fighting battles on behalf of God's people. Similarly, by living for Jesus, our words can inspire others, and our decisions can oppose wrongful actions.

Christian girls are also like the seraphim, special angels who worship around God's throne, saying, "**Holy, Holy, Holy.**"

These angels cover themselves in holiness to show respect and honor for the Lord. From great-grandmother to grandmother, and from grandmother to your mother, Christian women have passed down the wisdom of dressing in a way that pleases Jesus.

They teach that true beauty comes from the heart, but it also shows in how you present yourself.

Now, here's something to consider: **Are you more respected and liked when you dress neatly, modestly, and in a pleasing manner**, or when you wear loud, wild, or attention-seeking clothing? People tend to trust and admire those who seem to respect themselves.

When you dress in a way that honors Jesus, it's like dressing like the angels in heaven, pure, bright, and beautiful in their simplicity. But if you dress carelessly or in a way that confuses others about your faith, people might not take you seriously.

Which one do you think makes Jesus smile? We should listen to our parents.

If you're unsure, consider this: **What would your grandma or your mother recommend**? They've lived longer and have seen what kinds of choices bring respect and blessings. Their advice is a gift. Listening to them is a way of showing, **"I care about what's best for me."**

Christian parents want the best for you, just like Jesus does. They might not always explain everything right away, but they have more experience than you. And Jesus, who knows everything, can help you become more popular, more liked, and more admired than anyone else, if you follow His ways.

True popularity stems from being trustworthy, kind, and respectful, rather than from wearing the latest trend. When you learn to dress in a way that is appropriate and pleasing to God, you demonstrate that you belong to Him. It's not about being "old-fashioned" or "boring," *it's about saying, "I know who I am, and I'm proud to belong to Jesus."*

Some kids ask, "**Why don't Christians get tattoos**?" One reason is that our bodies are a gift from God. *They are like His temple, a holy place where His Spirit lives.* We want to care for that temple, not cover it with marks that last forever. **God made you wonderful just as you are, and you don't need to change His masterpiece.**

So, remember this: how you dress and care for yourself is part of the message you convey to the world. It shows people what you value and who you follow. When you choose clothing, actions, and habits that honor Jesus, you're walking in the footsteps of angels, pure, strong, and faithful. And that's something to be proud of every day. Your family will always be proud of who you are as a Christian.

Heavenly Father,

Our Father in heaven, hallowed be your name. Your kingdom come, your will be done, on earth as it is in heaven.

Thank You for loving me so much that You came to show us the Father. You said, *"Anyone who has seen Me has seen the Father"* (John 14:9), and You told us to *let our light shine before others so they may see You in me.*

Help me to remember that I represent You everywhere I go, at school, at home, at the park, online, or even in another country. Let my words be kind, my actions be good, and the way I dress bring You honor.

Make me like the angels in heaven, like Gabriel, bringing good messages, and like Michael, standing firm for what is right. Help me be like the seraphim who worship You in holiness, showing respect in everything they do, because I belong to You.

Thank You for the wisdom of my parents, grandparents, and family who teach me how to live and dress in ways that please You. Please help me to listen to them and trust their advice, knowing they want the best for me.

Show me that true beauty comes from the heart, as well as in how I present myself. Keep me from wanting to follow trends that take my focus off You. Instead, let my life be filled with kindness, respect, and joy that comes from You alone.

Lord, thank You for making my body Your temple. Help me take care of it, protect it, and be happy with the way You created me. I am your masterpiece; you are my God.

Let my choices, how I speak, act, and dress, tell the world that I belong to You. Make me strong and faithful, walking like the angels who serve You day and night.

May my light shine so brightly that when people see me, they will see Your love, Your kindness, and Your truth.

You are my friend, and I will always be yours.

In Jesus' name I pray, Amen.

Thank You for Reading!

Dear friend,

We hope you enjoyed discovering how special you are to Jesus.

He loves you more than you can imagine — today and every day!

Jesus said: *"I call all children my friends, for the kingdom of heaven belongs to them."*

If you want to learn more about Jesus, talk to Him in prayer and share His love with others.

With love and prayers from: Gabe, Isaiah, and Gershom.